LIVING WITH MODERN SCULPTURE

Patrick J. Kelleher

LIVING WITH MODERN SCULPTURE

The John B. Putnam, Jr., Memorial Collection
Princeton University

The Art Museum, Princeton University
in association with
Princeton University Press

Designed by James Wageman
Set in type by U.S. Lithograph, Inc.
Printed by Village Craftsmen

Jacket and page 34: Pablo Picasso, *Head of a Woman*
(*Tête de Femme*), cat. no. 15

Frontispiece: Louise Nevelson, *Atmosphere and
Environment X*, cat. no. 11

Pages 6–7: Gaston Lachaise, *Floating Figure*, cat. no. 6

Photographs
COLOR: Clem Fiori, Blawenberg, N.J.
BLACK AND WHITE: Jörg P. Anders, Berlin, 114 top right;
Marie E. Bellis, Hopewell, N.J., 98;
Clem Fiori, Blawenberg, N.J., 50, 69, 75, 90;
J. Henry Laboratories, Princeton, N.J., 102;
Kroeze Fotograaf, Rotterdam, 21; Robin Lloyd, 123;
Robert E. Mates, New York, 20; Robert T. Matthews,
Trenton, N.J., 129; Beryl Sokoloff, New York, frontispiece,
6–7, 34, 38 right, 43 right, 58, 70 top left and bottom,
74, 86, 94 left, 103, 110 left, 115, 119, 128;
SPADEM, Paris / VAGA, New York, 27; Ezra Stoller © Esto,
New York, 82; Taylor & Dull, Inc., New York, 38 left,
42 left, 43 right, 47, 63, 66, 78, 79, 83, 118 bottom;
James Wageman, Princeton, N.J., 110 bottom right

Library of Congress Catalog Number 81-80639
ISBN 0-691-03897-X

Published by The Art Museum, Princeton University,
in association with Princeton University Press,
Princeton, New Jersey 08540
In the United Kingdom, Princeton University Press,
Guildford, Surrey

Contents

Message from the President *by William G. Bowen*   6

Foreword *by Allen Rosenbaum*   8

Preface   9

Lieutenant John B. Putnam, Jr., 1921–1944   11

The History and Formation of a Collection   12

Introduction *by Hugh M. Davies*   16

The John B. Putnam, Jr., Memorial Collection   35

1 Reg Butler, *The Bride*   36

2 Alexander Calder, *Five Disks: One Empty*   40

3 Sir Jacob Epstein, *Professor Albert Einstein*   44

4 Naum Gabo, *Spheric Theme*   48

5 Michael David Hall, *Mastodon VI*   52

6 Gaston Lachaise, *Floating Figure*   56

7 Jacques Lipchitz, *Song of the Vowels*   60

8 Clement Meadmore, *Upstart 2*   64

9 Henry Moore, *Oval with Points*   68

10 Masayuki Nagare, *Stone Riddle*   72

11 Louise Nevelson, *Atmosphere and Environment X*   76

12 Isamu Noguchi, *White Sun*   80

13 Eduardo Paolozzi, *Marok-Marok-Miosa*   84

14 Antoine Pevsner, *Construction in the Third and Fourth Dimension*   88

15 Pablo Picasso, *Head of a Woman*   92

16 Arnaldo Pomodoro, *Sphere VI*   96

17 George Rickey, *Two Planes Vertical Horizontal II*   100

18 George Segal, *Abraham and Isaac: In Memory of May 4, 1970, Kent State University*   104

19 David Smith, *Cubi XIII*   108

20 Tony Smith, *Moses*   112

21 Kenneth Snelson, *Northwood II*   116

Map Showing Locations of the Sculptures   120

Appendix 1   Conservation of Outdoor Sculpture *by Youngja Lee Kim*   122

Appendix 2   Picasso's Collaborator: Carl Nesjar   128

Notes   130

Selected Checklist of Other Twentieth-Century Sculptures at Princeton University   137

Bibliography   138

Message from the President

The publication of a catalogue on the John B. Putnam, Jr., Memorial Collection is a very special event, not only because the collection deserves to be properly recorded, but also because the occasion provides us with an opportunity to recognize the degree to which the collection enhances and enriches the life of the University.

Princeton is extraordinarily proud of the Putnam Collection. It is one of the country's most dramatic permanent displays of major twentieth-century sculpture, containing, as it does, superb examples of sculpture by the finest contemporary sculptors in the world. And it is a tribute to the vision of the donor that he enabled Princeton to be one of the first university campuses in this country where one could see, study, and enjoy a group of distinctive works in a medium in which some of the most exciting developments in modern art are now occuring.

In a residential university such as Princeton, the campus, the physical characteristics of the place, have a pervasive effect. Lewis Thomas, Class of 1933, in a speech given on Alumni Day 1981, described Princeton as having "the look, and the feel, of an institution deliberately designed for *thinking* and kept that way through the years." Most assuredly, the Putnam Collection is a major addition to Princeton's cultural resources, offering an exceptional opportunity for learning that exposes the untutored to the best in modern art at the same time as it delights the most sophisticated art scholar. But, even more, the collection is a source of vitality, a reminder of the possibilities of form, for each of us as we walk on the campus. It is, I think, the ideal complement to the natural beauty of this University, an added pleasure in the daily lives of each of us.

William G. Bowen

Foreword

Accustomed as we are today to sculpture gardens and the incorporation of works of art in any responsible architectural undertaking, we must acknowledge the vision and breadth that the gift of the John B. Putnam, Jr., Memorial Collection in 1968 represented. Although the collection has become an integral part of the campus at Princeton, these sculptures — even those placed along the most well-worn paths — continue to provide us with a sense of lively stimulation, aesthetic pleasure, and pride.

Although the collection was conceived as a balanced, integral whole, with works by both established masters of twentieth-century sculpture and innovative but accomplished younger artists, there have been additional gifts of sculpture to the University because of the continuing interest of Mildred Andrews Putnam and Peter Putnam through the Mildred Andrews Fund and the John B. Putnam, Jr., Foundation. In 1979, the University received a gift of George Segal's *Abraham and Isaac: In Memory of May 4, 1970, Kent State University*. In the same year, the Mildred Andrews Fund provided matching funds for an NEA purchase grant for the acquisition of works by American sculptors, with which *Public Table* by Scott Burton and *Gnomon's Parade* by Christopher Wilmarth were purchased. In 1981, the Third World Center at Princeton University was presented with *Trope* by Hugh Harrell. The most recent gift to the University has been a bronze cast of the final study for the head of the figure of Balzac for the *Monument to Balzac* by Auguste Rodin. While these gifts are not part of the original John B. Putnam, Jr., Memorial Collection, the Segal has been included in the catalogue. Such continuing gifts are consistent with the spirit of the original gift and have kept it a vital and open enterprise.

The person most continuously associated with this project is Patrick Joseph Kelleher, Graduate School Class of 1947. Director of the Museum at the time the gift was presented to the University, he was intimately involved in the selection and placement of the sculptures. He is, of course, the author of this catalogue, which will serve as a companion handbook to a tour of the collection. We are very much in his debt for his dedication and labors on behalf of this project. It is with special pride too that we could turn to Hugh Davies, Graduate School Class of 1970, now the director of the Art Gallery, University of Massachusetts at Amherst, for the very fine introductory historical essay to the catalogue.

Thomas P.F. Hoving, Class of 1953 and Graduate School Class of 1960, a member of the original Selections Committee for the Putnam Collection, remains a valued and supportive consultant when new works of sculpture are sponsored by the same donor, as in the case of the NEA purchase grant.

Virginia Wageman, formerly director of publications at The Art Museum, has supervised this publication since its inception, and Jill Guthrie has seen the catalogue through the final stages of production. Robert Lafond, Registrar, provided the entry for the George Segal sculpture.

Youngja Kim, a specialist in the conservation of sculpture, has been occupied for some years with the problems of conservation and maintenance presented by outdoor sculpture, of a frequency and magnitude not always anticipated when a work is first installed. Her reports are included in an appendix to this catalogue. Her research has resulted in measures and methods of the greatest value in this field, and we are grateful to the NEA for their support of her work at Princeton.

One of the nicest developments inspired by the Putnam Collection is the annual Princeton Sculpture Run, complete with T-shirts, initiated by Professor Marilyn McCully of the Department of Art and Archaeology. Every spring, those so moved participate in a run from sculpture to sculpture with pauses for remarks on the individual works. It is happily an event that requires more spirit than endurance, and it is a delightful index of the way in which the John B. Putnam, Jr., Memorial Collection continues to be a fresh and vital stimulus to our lives in Princeton.

Allen Rosenbaum
Director

Preface

Early in the fall of 1969, the final version of Jacques Lipchitz's *Song of the Vowels* became the first of the John B. Putnam, Jr., Memorial Collection of twentieth-century sculptures to be placed on the campus of Princeton University. All the works in the collection have long since found sites on this campus, where parklike grounds and trees frame an architectural tradition bridging more than two centuries. The Putnam sculptures have settled into the terrain so successfully that it is now difficult to recall a time when they were not an integral part of it. They attract their own responsive audience and have gained a devoted following not only among the University family and the Princeton community, but also in the world beyond.

This monograph is designed to serve as catalogue, handbook, and guide to an exceptional collection. It aspires to provide a basic reference catholic enough to encompass the needs and interests of a diverse public, whose members have in common a desire to experience more fully the energy, originality, and meaning of these remarkable works of art.

For ease of reference, the artists represented in the Putnam Memorial Collection appear in alphabetical order and are numbered accordingly. A checklist of other University-owned twentieth-century sculpture appears as an appendix to this monograph.

Essays dealing with the collection owe much to those artists, their families and dealers, and to the scholars of their work who generously sent statements and information for use in this catalogue. The author wishes to express particular appreciation to them all for adding so richly to the documentation of the Putnam sculptures and enhancing this publication materially through their perceptive observations and knowledge. The cooperation of publishers, authors, and museums in granting authorization to reproduce passages of text and collateral photographs is also gratefully acknowledged.

Two documentary films have been produced to supplement the photographic record of the Putnam sculptures. "Sculpture in the Open," created for New Jersey Public Broadcasting by Hugh and Suzanne Johnston of Princeton, examines the works by Picasso, Lipchitz, Calder, Tony Smith, and Henry Moore, and has appeared nationally on Public Broadcasting Service channels. "Tête de Femme" (with narrative commentary by Carl Nesjar) was produced by Beryl Sokoloff and records the construction of Picasso's cast-concrete sculpture. The Putnam Memorial Collection has also had international exposure on Voice of America broadcasts.

Throughout the period when the sculptures were being selected and installed on the campus, Robert F. Goheen, then president of the University, was an ardently involved supporter of the project. Acquisition of the Putnam Collection for Princeton must rank high among Dr. Goheen's many outstanding contributions to the University during his tenure as president, and owes much to his sense of personal commitment. His successor, William G. Bowen, has perpetuated this policy of concerned interest, and has delegated overall supervision and maintenance of the collection to the director of The Art Museum of the University.

The Art Museum, designed as a teaching museum, is a treasure house of occidental and oriental art from antiquity to the present. Among its works of twentieth-century sculpture are several that complement those to be seen outdoors on the campus, including the maquettes for the sculptures in the Putnam Collection by Calder, Meadmore, Moore, Nevelson, Tony Smith, and Snelson.

Particular acknowledgment is due to Jeremiah A. Farrington, Jr., former assistant to President Goheen and now assistant dean of the School of Engineering and Applied Science, who, as the representative of two presidents, was charged with the coordination of all administrative activities connected with the program. Similarly, John P. Moran, one time vice-president for facilities at the University, orchestrated the technical considerations of siting, installation, landscaping, and the physical care of the sculptures. These gentlemen were indispensable for the success of the project.

The late Michael Rapuano, consulting landscape

architect for the University, gave invaluable counsel in the location of many of the sculptures and the landscaping of their sites. Carl F. Brauer, a deputy to Mr. Moran, aided immeasurably in the work of installation, labeling, and subsequent inspections for condition of the sculptures. John A. Wheeler, formerly Joseph Henry Professor in the Department of Physics, made helpful recommendations on numerous occasions and also selected the quotations for the Niels Bohr memorial inscriptions associated with the sculpture by Antoine Pevsner.

In addition to those formal duties already acknowledged, Dean Farrington's sustained personal interest in the project and the assistance he has given the author call for special acknowledgment. Mary Laing and Virginia Wageman synthesized the publication and my debt to them for their many kindnesses, patience, and understanding is limitless.

Mrs. John B. Putnam, Sr., of Cleveland, mother of Lieutenant Putnam, has visited the campus on several occasions and encouraged all those involved in the project by her dedicated and enthusiastic inter-est. The task accomplished by the Selections Committee appointed by President Goheen to bring about this assembly of modern sculpture for the Putnam Memorial and for Princeton speaks for itself in the monuments chosen.

Final words of gratitude and appreciation are reserved for the anonymous donor whose farsighted generosity made the Putnam Memorial Collection a reality. If we substitute the designation "university" for "church" in the statement of Bishop Virginio Dondeo on the installation in 1970 of modern bronze doors in the cathedral of Orvieto, Italy, we will come close, I believe, to the heart of the impulse that prompted this exceptional gift to Princeton University as a memorial for John B. Putnam, Jr.: "A church is not something to be put in a museum under glass. It is a living thing, and each century makes its contribution . . . so that it becomes a continuing expression of the faith of everyone who worships there."

Patrick J. Kelleher

John B. Putnam, Jr., was born in Cleveland, Ohio, on January 20, 1921. After early education in schools in Cleveland and in Switzerland, he entered Princeton University in the fall of 1940. Leaving the University at the end of his sophomore year to enlist in the U.S. Army Air Force, he received his wings in late 1943 and was sent to the European theater of operations in April 1944 as a pursuit pilot. Named flight leader of a Thunderbolt fighter squadron, Lieutenant Putnam flew nine combat hours over the Normandy beaches on D-Day, June 6, 1944, and had completed fifty-three combat missions before crashing to his death in England on July 19, 1944, at age twenty-three. He wrote in his diary: "Courage is not the lack of fear but the ability to face it." During the last two and one-half months of combat flying before his death, John Putnam was awarded the Air Medal, six silver-leaf clusters and, posthumously, the Distinguished Flying Cross "for extraordinary achievement and heroism in aerial combat."

Early in March 1968, President Robert F. Goheen announced Princeton University's receipt of a singular gift: a fund approximating one million dollars that would, in his words, "bring a group of magnificent works of art to the campus, enriching Princeton's cultural resources in the arts, and prove to be of advancing benefit down through the years."

Presented by an anonymous donor, the gift was designated as a memorial to Lieutenant John B. Putnam, Jr., of Cleveland, Ohio, a member of the Class of 1945 killed in action in World War II. The memorial to Lieutenant Putnam—who was characterized by a close associate as "something of a woodland creature" and a "forger of the new freedom"—was designed to fulfill a congruent belief by the anonymous donor that modern sculpture is "becoming a symbol of a new creative freedom in man."

Accompanying the gift were carefully deliberated guidelines that contained some unusual features. The sculptures acquired for the memorial were not to be placed in The Art Museum of Princeton University or in a sculpture garden. Rather, they were to be installed outdoors in prominent sites throughout the campus, so that students and the community would experience these works of art casually and in the normal course of daily living.

Another stipulation was that not all the selected works be abstract and that a large number should interpret the human form in the idiom of modern sculpture. Quality, too, was a major consideration: "Outstanding works by masters in a lesser category are certainly to be preferred to lesser works by greater masters." Finally, the donor expressed the hope that original drawings and maquettes of the sculptures be included with the purchases and kept in The Art Museum to augment the scholarly value of the memorial.

Having consulted initially with Dr. Sherman E. Lee, director of the Cleveland Museum of Art and a friend of the Putnam family, the donor proposed as a guide a list of some thirty, diversified "masters of modern sculpture" whose works potentially would be suitable for acquisition. It was, however, under-

stood that a number of these artists might be *hors concours* because their works would be more appropriate in medium and scale for museum exhibition than for open-air installation. Sought-after works also might not be obtainable because they already had been acquired elsewhere. Nonetheless, it is of interest that of the twelve artists listed by the donor in the first three most desired categories, seven are now represented by major works in the Putnam Memorial.

To fulfill the donor's aspirations and to assemble the collection, President Goheen designated a four-man advisory Committee on Selections drawn from alumni of Princeton University with professional knowledge of the fine arts. The members of the committee were Alfred H. Barr, Jr. '22 (M.A. '23, Litt. D. '49), director emeritus of the Museum of Modern Art, New York; Thomas P. F. Hoving '53 (Ph.D. '60), then director of the Metropolitan Museum of Art, New York; the late William M. Milliken '11 (Hon. M.F.A. '42), formerly director emeritus of the Cleveland Museum of Art; and the present writer (M.F.A. '42; Ph.d. '47), then director of The Art Museum, Princeton University, and Professor of Art and Archaeology. Jeremiah A. Farrington '41, assistant to the president, and John P. Moran '51, then director for grounds and buildings, served in an advisory capacity to the Selections Committee, representing the University.

The initial meeting of the committee was held in late March 1968. Goals and procedures for acquisitions were established, and possible locations for the sculptures were considered. The search for the sculptures themselves began shortly thereafter.

By early 1969, President Goheen had approved the committee's recommendations to secure seven works: Jacques Lipchitz's *Song of the Vowels* (in the early stages of casting); David Smith's *Cubi XIII*; Arnaldo Pomodoro's *Sphere VI*; Michael Hall's *Mastodon VI*; Eduardo Paolozzi's *Marok-Marok-Miosa*; Tony Smith's *Moses*; and Louise Nevelson's *Atmosphere and Environment X*. The last two were still in the maquette stage. Authorization was also given to proceed with negotiations for works by Pablo Picasso, Antoine Pevsner, and Alexander Calder. By mid-April, *Floating Figure* by Gaston Lachaise, yet to be cast, and *Oval with Points* by Henry Moore, in the maquette stage, had been gained for the collection.

The committee was able to report in the spring of 1969 that the casting of the Lipchitz bronze was nearing completion, that the Lachaise and Tony Smith sculptures would be available for installation by summer or early fall, and that the David Smith would be delivered to Princeton at the end of the year after traveling in a major retrospective exhibition of the artist's work. The Moore and Pevsner bronzes would require another year to execute, and Picasso would be approached in the fall to approve translating the maquette of his 1962 *Head of a Woman* into a monumental sculpture for Princeton.

By December 1969, the sculptures of Lipchitz, Tony Smith, Paolozzi, Pomodoro, Lachaise, David Smith, and Hall were installed on the campus. Works by Moore, Pevsner, and Nevelson were in the process of casting or fabrication and expected for delivery during the coming year. Picasso had given approval for the construction of *Head of a Woman*, with work scheduled to commence in the spring.

During the early months of 1970, Reg Butler's *The Bride*, Isamu Noguchi's *White Sun*, and Kenneth Snelson's *Northwood II* were added to the collection, to be joined, in late October, by Sir Jacob Epstein's bronze bust of Albert Einstein, one of the last casts of this notable portrait not already in a public collection.

The year 1971 saw the on-site execution by Carl Nesjar of Picasso's *Head of a Woman*, an operation that fascinated the Princeton community for months. Calder's stabile, *Five Disks: One Empty*, Moore's *Oval with Points*, and Nevelson's *Atmosphere and Environment X* were given their final locations. Clement Meadmore's *Upstart 2* was purchased, and negotiations with Naum Gabo to execute a sculpture for the collection were begun.

Between 1972 and 1974, the acquisitions and in-stallations were completed. In 1972, George Rickey's *Two Planes Vertical Horizontal II* and Masayuki Nagare's *Stone Riddle* were installed. Pevsner's *Construction in the Third and Fourth Dimension* was located in the interior court of Jadwin Hall and dedicated additionally as a memorial to the noted Danish scientist Niels Bohr. The Selections Committee asked Gabo to execute *Spheric Theme* for the collection. In 1973, the sculptures of Meadmore, Snelson, Noguchi, and David Smith were installed in congenial sites, and finally, in December 1974, in the presence of Gabo, *Spheric Theme* was placed on the green of 1879 Hall to serve as a fitting capstone for an enlightened gift and a lasting memorial to Lieutenant John B. Putnam, Jr., of the Class of 1945.

Endowed with a parklike landscape, magnificent trees, and buildings of notable architectural interest, the Princeton campus theoretically offered minimum challenge in determining locations for the Putnam sculptures. On the contrary, however, every site had to be chosen from several different possibilities, each of which offered the means to enhance an individual work.

A serious attempt was made to respect the donor's wish that sculptures in the collection be readily accessible for an alternately mobile and sedentary university population. In this fashion, living with outdoor sculpture could become a *modus vivendi*. Consequently, preference in siting was given to centers of public activity and traffic, for example, areas contiguous to Firestone Library, the Chapel, and The Art Museum; to areas combining multiple disciplines, such as the mathematics/physics and the engineering/applied sciences complexes; to communal and dormitory housing; and in the case of Nevelson's *Atmosphere and Environment X*, to a placement on Princeton's main artery, Nassau Street, establishing a bridge for common experience between town and gown.

But suitable locations were also sought for the smaller scaled and less assertive works of art that court private rather than public attention. Their special kind of expressive vitality can be appreciated best through initial discovery attended by surprise and, subsequently, by relaxed observation. Butler's *The Bride*, Lachaise's *Floating Figure*, and the abstractions of Nagare and Pomodoro, conceived as they are in human scale, found compatible settings in interior courtyards or on greens of academic buildings and living facilities. These sculptures are contemplated frequently through classroom or dormitory windows in contrast to those viewed by strollers or students on the move. Treated similarly in installation were the indoor sculptures, Noguchi's *White Sun* and Epstein's *Professor Albert Einstein*, which were placed respectively in the busy entrance lobbies of Firestone and Fine libraries.

Among the relatively few problems that occurred during installation of the Putnam sculptures was a dialogue between the Princeton zoning board and the University over the proper location and classification of Nevelson's *Atmosphere and Environment X*. This 16-foot-high, geometric composition, consisting of boxlike elements made of Cor-Ten steel, was placed initially several feet closer than its present site to the sidewalk on the University side of Nassau Street. Princeton's zoning board cited the installation for creating a violation of local building codes, characterizing the sculpture "a building" that breached ordinance by its placement. The University contended that the Nevelson was a work of art rather than an edifice. The zoning board countered by agreeing to consider an amendment allowing the sculpture to remain if a more precise definition were submitted that would clarify the distinction between a construction that constituted a building and one that was a work of art. Meanwhile, Meadmore's giant *Upstart 2*, scheduled for location in front of the Engineering Quadrangle but regarded by the zoning board as being in the same technical limbo as the Nevelson, languished for months at Lippincott, Inc., fabricators of the sculpture.

Fortunately, in the interim, the Selections Committee recommended a change of location for the Nevelson to a site some feet back from the street, on a mounded green covering a recently completed underground addition to Firestone Library. Aesthetically the new position was a preferable one, improving the visibility of the sculpture for both the University and the community. A similar accommodation in footage and direction of thrust subsequently insured the siting as planned for *Upstart 2*.

Far more serious was a tragic accident that occurred on June 3, 1970. During a trial installation of Calder's massive steel sculpture, *Five Disks: One Empty*, on the plaza of the Fine/Jadwin complex, steel cables of a crane lifting the 4½-ton stabile into position snapped, collapsing the boom and killing two steel riggers, Edwin A. Dillon and Robert J. Fuccello. As a consequence, the sculpture was retired to storage for a year until lessened anguish enabled it to be reinstalled on the plaza in August 1971. A plaque commemorating the two men is attached to a wall of the balustrade approaching the stabile from Washington Road.

Installations of the sculptures by Lipchitz, Nevelson, Moore, Meadmore, Tony Smith, Rickey, and Gabo—the last four artists were present to supervise the siting of their works—occurred when the University was in session and consequently drew sizable audiences of students and faculty. The interest and enthusiasm generated on these occasions were infectious. The installation of Moore's *Oval with Points* on the green between West College and Stanhope Hall, for example, drew President Goheen from his office in adjacent Nassau Hall to exercise his presidential prerogative by directing the swinging crane's placement of the 2½-ton bronze. The sculptor himself, incidentally, had visited the campus early in the project to discuss the possibilities of a major sculpture for the Putnam Memorial and to inspect potential sites.

The installation that created the greatest dramatic interest was undoubtedly Nesjar's construction in cast concrete of Picasso's *Head of a Woman* on the green before the entrance to The Art Museum and McCormick Hall. While the monumental work was in the process of execution over a period of some five months, Nesjar conducted a unique, outdoor seminar for an audience drawn from the University and local communities. During intervals from his work on the sculpture, the artist endured a bombardment of queries from students and other sidewalk viewers, and with patience and pedagogical finesse turned the act of construction into an educational experience. The opportunity to participate in the re-creation, on a monumental scale, of a felicitous work of imagination by a twentieth-century master is but one instance of the contribution the Putnam Memorial Collection has made to the continuing process of education at Princeton.

In its deliberations, the Selections Committee paid close attention to the source, uniqueness, or number of authorized casts or editions of sculptures purchased for the collection. With the exception of the Epstein bust of Einstein (bought at auction from Christie's of London), all the works were obtained directly from the artist, the artist's estate, or an authorized dealer. Several sculptures offered on the international art market were avoided because of doubts concerning their pedigree or provenance.

In the accepted tradition, still commonly practiced in modern sculpture, the artist determines whether a work is to be unique or executed in an edition of predetermined number. Of the twenty-one sculptures acquired for the Putnam Memorial, ten are unique and ten exist in editions whose authorized numbers vary from two through eight; in the case of the Epstein, the size of the edition planned by the sculptor is not certain. Seventeen of the works were either executed by the artists themselves, or were cast or fabricated for Princeton under their direct supervision. The Pevsner and Lachaise bronzes (both posthumous strikes) were cast from original plasters through arrangements made with the widow and the estate, respectively, of the artists. Picasso gave his personal approval for the creation of the unique version of *Head of a Woman* at Princeton, and designated Nesjar as the executant.

For this guidebook, care has been taken to establish, when possible, the owners and locations of other known, authorized versions of the sculptures in the Putnam Memorial. This information is incorporated into the separate essays on the artists and their works in the collection.

It was the conviction of the anonymous donor who established the fund for the creation of the John B. Putnam, Jr., Memorial Collection at Princeton that "the most exciting and important development in the art of our times is occurring in sculpture." Only the passage of time itself can prove the validity of this belief, but certain it is that sculpture has experienced a remarkable renaissance in the twentieth century. So vigorous has the medium become that it can be said with assurance that it would be possible to assemble at least two additional collections comparable in size and quality to the Putnam Memorial with scarcely any duplication of artists.

During the last half-generation, exceptional collections of modern sculpture have proliferated throughout the country in museums, sculpture gardens, parks, civic centers, and regional communities extending from the Franklin D. Murphy Sculpture Garden at the University of California at Los Angeles to the Mall of the State Capitol in Albany, New York. Parallelling these, there have been an extraordinary number of temporary exhibitions and civic projects featuring both indoor and outdoor sculpture. Among these evidences of the contemporary vitality of the medium, the Putnam Collection enjoys a unique position in that its donor conceived of modern sculpture as an essential element in the educational process, leading to an ultimate enrichment of everyday living for all. Like books to which a person becomes attached through constant and informal contact, these sculptures in the Putnam Memorial are exerting a comparable influence on the spirits, minds, and formative experiences of the young, on whom the future of this imperfect world must rely.

Introduction
Hugh M. Davies

The history of modern sculpture can be seen to begin with a rejection—the refusal of the Société des Gens de Lettres to accept the image of *Balzac* (1897) which they had commissioned Auguste Rodin to sculpt. Symbolically this marked a separation of sculpture from its traditional patrons. Sculptors were now free to experiment in private and ultimately to find new patrons. The evolution of modern sculpture is a history of expanding options, options made possible by the revitalizing and often radical innovations of such key figures as Rodin, Picasso, Brancusi, Gabo, Giacometti, and Moore. In discovering and exploring these new possibilities, twentieth-century sculptors have drawn on the traditions of painting and architecture as liberally as on their own medium's past.

   The great progenitor of modern sculpture, Auguste Rodin, was benevolently disposed toward the tradition of his medium. Rodin worked most often in the modelled clay and plaster cast in bronze, and dealt primarily with traditional figurative subjects commemorating great men, significant events of history, and religious trends—in *Balzac*, *The Burghers of Calais*, and *The Gates of Hell*. The intensity with which he probed his subjects is reflected in the divergence of his sculptures from the characterless idealization of works by many of his contemporaries. The figure of *Balzac* was rejected as a gross caricature of the illustrious literary figure that it commemorates. *The Gates of Hell*, intended as a portal for the never built museum of decorative arts in Paris, swells and subsides with the tormented writhing of its inhabitants in a bleakly modern interpretation of Dante's *Inferno*. *Eve*, originally conceived by Rodin as one of the figures in *The Gates of Hell*, was sculpted life-size and exhibited in the Salon of 1898 with its base buried in the dirt floor, a gesture intended to intensify the impression of reality. This impulse toward realism had been manifest in *Man with a Broken Nose* of 1864, rejected by the Salon early in Rodin's career. Rodin nonetheless remained essentially within the tradition of sculpture in his use

Auguste Rodin, *Monument to Balzac*, 1897–98, bronze (cast 1954), 8′10″ (H).
The Museum of Modern Art, New York.
Presented in memory of Curt Valentin by his friends

Auguste Rodin, *The Burghers of Calais*, 1886, bronze, 82½″ × 95″ × 78″.
Hirshhorn Museum and Sculpture Garden, Smithsonian Institution

Auguste Rodin, *Mask of the Man with the Broken Nose*,
1964, bronze, 12½″ × 7½″ × 6½″.
Hirshhorn Museum and Sculpture Garden,
Smithsonian Institution

Opposite left: Alexander Archipenko, *Walking Woman*,
1912, bronze, 26⅜″ (H). Perls Galleries, New York

Opposite right: Pablo Picasso, *Guitar*, 1912,
sheet metal and wire, 30½″ × 13⅛″ × 7⅝″.
The Museum of Modern Art, New York. Gift of the artist

of materials, his choice of subject, and his relation
to patrons; among his artistic forebears were the
giants of Renaissance sculpture, Donatello and
Michelangelo.

In the twentieth century, the nature of public art
in general and public sculpture in particular has
changed. Rodin's testy relationship with his patrons
signalled a period of reevaluation of the role and
nature of patronage of public art. Indeed in the
earliest decades of this century, art came increasingly
to answer to artistic criteria more readily than to
patrons' whims. Accordingly, the commemorative
function of public sculpture became optional, and
such mundane subject matter as the bottles and gui-
tars of Cubist still lifes provided the foil for some of

the most significant innovations of the medium. Not
surprisingly, many of the great, innovative works of
the early twentieth century were executed as "private" works, often in small scale.

In line with the development of abstract art,
modern sculpture often bears little relation to the
figure or to recognizable objects. Instead, much
modern sculpture is strictly non-objective, often aligned with architecture in its formal rhythms and
references. Despite the dominance of non-figurative
work, the figure survives, albeit radically transformed
by twentieth-century concerns.

It was in fact within the tradition of figurative
sculpture that many of the most significant early
breakthroughs in the medium were made. Not only

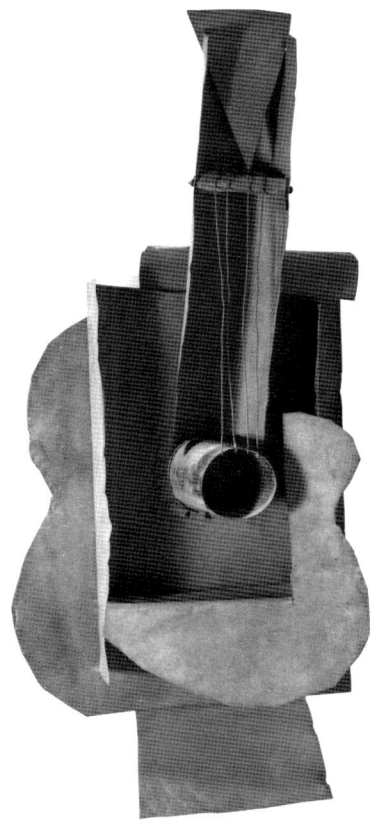

were the base and pedestal called into question in Rodin's *Eve*, but in *The Burghers of Calais*, the figures wander about independently and have little more unity than do a group of people milling about a town square. Seen in this way, the intervals of space between the figures become a significant element,[1] auguring the crucial role of space in Cubist and Constructivist sculpture and eerily anticipating the extraordinarily activated spaces of Giacometti— spaces that erode the figures who inhabit them. So too the crucial penetration of sculptural mass was decisively accomplished in Alexander Archipenko's *Walking Woman* of 1912.

Despite the progressive thrust of Rodin's realist aspirations, his impressionistic surfaces, and expres-

sionistic rendering of figures, he never questioned the concept of sculpture as mass. Picasso and his fellow Cubists, taking their lead from Cézanne, broke the dictum that rendering the world on a two-dimensional surface according to Renaissance perspective was the goal of painting. Picasso extended this challenge to the discipline of sculpture in works that were personal experiments created on an intimate scale rather than heroic statements intended for public view. So, for example, one of the most inspirational works of the century, Picasso's *Guitar* of 1912, was humble in subject and small in scale. Rather than conceiving of the musical instrument as a three-dimensional mass of wood, Picasso recognized it to be a series of flat and curved

Naum Gabo, *Column*, 1923, plastic, wood, metal, 41″ (H).
The Solomon R. Guggenheim Museum, New York

proportions while the form is reduced to three essential geometric elements. The neck is a simple cylinder that supports a head reduced to two planes of the face. The rendering of the features and the disinterest in the mass of the head reveal the influence of African masks, which had inspired Picasso during his Cubist period.

Throughout his innovative career Picasso's work remained rooted in the seen world. However abstract his images, a figurative or still-life source is always recognizable. Yet his early Cubist works served as the inspiration for the purely abstract or non-objective work of the Constructivists. Vladimir Tatlin, seeing the *Guitar* and other constructions by Picasso on a visit to Paris in 1913, was inspired by the innovative definition of space and the possibilities of non-traditional materials. This same year, after returning to Russia, he created reliefs of wood and metal to be suspended in the corners of rooms, and introduced the word "Constructivism" in reference to his new sculptural approach. He and his Russian Constructivist colleagues Naum Gabo and Antoine Pevsner sought to create a new twentieth-century art investigating space, movement, and time without representation, and embracing transparent materials as a means of defining space without creating mass. Such materials as glass, plastic, wood, wire, and metal seemed appropriate for a new art form that rejected sentimental or subjective personal reference, and aligned itself with the postrevolutionary vision. Drawing on scientific and philosophical concepts rather than extant objects, Gabo and Pevsner defined space by articulating flat and curved planes.

By 1922 the Russian government had suppressed the Constructivist movement and Gabo and Pevsner had left their homeland. In 1923 Gabo created his *Column* of glass, metal, plastic, and wood, rendering space palpable as he "edged" and "surrounded" it with geometric shapes and transparent planes. It anticipates the concerns of such large-scale, outdoor works as his eighty-foot-high *Rotterdam Construction* of 1957 and *Spheric Theme* of 1973–1974 at Princeton.

planes surrounding and defining space. In translating this concept into a sculptural statement he rejected both traditional materials and techniques. Rather he assembled sheets of metal, defining the voids or space more actively than the surfaces. The sound hole becomes a tubular volume and the wire strings describe yet another open plane. Much as an axonometric drawing gives us more information about a structure than an architect's rendering, Picasso's sheet metal *Guitar* pointed the way for sculpture to deal with space rather than mass.

Picasso's *Head of a Woman*, constructed on the Princeton campus some sixty years later, reasserts qualities of Cubism discovered at the time of the *Guitar*. The bust of the woman is inflated to heroic

Naum Gabo, *Construction* in front of the Bijenkorf department store, 1957, steel, bronze, wire, freestone substructure, 85′ (H). Property of Mag. De Bijenkorf, Rotterdam, The Netherlands

Vladimir Tatlin,
*Monument to the
Third International,*
1919–20, wood, iron,
glass. Russian State
Museum, Leningrad

The most ambitious and optimistic project associated with Constructivism was Tatlin's commissioned proposal and model for the *Monument to the Third International* of 1920. The proposed sculpture was to be of a vast scale analogous to the Statue of Liberty. Tatlin's proposal was revolutionary in form but traditional in its humanitarian and commemorative intention. The never actualized structure would have been 1,300 feet high, and was intended to be a felicitous blend of architecture and sculpture, housing within its metal frames volumes of meeting rooms that would revolve.

This convergence of architecture and sculpture signalled a vital tendency of the twentieth century, reflected in the blurred distinction between the two media in such public structures as Eero Saarinen's St. Louis archway and Nicholas Schoffer's large-scale cybernetic towers (the first of which was erected at the Park of St. Cloud in 1954). Indeed, Schoffer's towers are considered sculptures, but are in fact just as architectural as is the tower of the engineer-architect Eiffel in Paris. In the same city, the Arc de Triomphe reiterates in nineteenth-century guise the merging of architecture and sculpture, since it is an archway used solely as a monument to Napoleon and a memorial to the unknown French soldier. Such an ambitious sculptural project as Alexander Liberman's entrance arch to the University of Pennsylvania (1976), is as much of an actual gateway as is the Brandenburg Gate or Michelangelo's Porta Pia. As architectural elements, Marcel Breuer's entry to the Whitney Museum and Le Corbusier's entry to the monastery of La Tourette are vestigial reworkings of formerly functional fortifications that now serve on a purely formal level as sculptural appendages. Such contemporary artists as George Trakas, Alice Adams, Alice Aycock, Mary Miss, and Richard Fleischner probe this realm of architectural-sculptural interaction by creating structures intended to be experienced as "architecture"—to be walked through, under, and around—and requiring the dimension of time so important to the original Constructivists.

Paralleling Picasso's Cubist redefinition of sculpture, Italian Futurists like Umberto Boccioni created such dynamic works as *Unique Forms of Continuity in Space* (1913). Though traditionally cast in bronze like Rodin's *Walking Man*, the sculpture's title alone points to a more ambitious purpose, and reflects the new liberties taken with the human form. Rather than seeking to render the figure's particular features, Boccioni was concerned with capturing a three-dimensional representation of motion. While Rodin conveyed movement by freezing the action at mid-stride, Boccioni presented the figure in a veritable wind-tunnel projection, extending blurred limbs into palpable, air-current eddies. The Futurists heralded the Machine Age and revelled in the potential force of the internal combustion engine. In Boccioni's heroic image of man in motion, the primitive streamlining of early automobiles is adapted to transform the figure into a human speed machine, a modern Mercury whose form melds with the surrounding space. As their adopted name conveys, the Futurists welcomed, rather indiscriminately, the advances of science and technology as they propelled mankind speedily toward the future.

While early Cubists tentatively faceted the human form, the Russian-born Alexander Archipenko, working in Paris in 1912, took the decisive step of subverting the mass of the human form. In his *Walking Woman*, he established a balance of positive and negative areas by hollowing out the head and torso. This diminutive work (26½ inches high) provides the precedent for Jacques Lipchitz's fenestrated *Song of the Vowels* (1931–1932), as well as for Henry Moore's subsequent hollowed-out, landscapelike reclining figures.

In connection with the desire to work with space rather than mass, the impulse toward new materials emerged in the teens from several different groups of artists. Aside from the Constructivists' and Cubists' use of new materials, Boccioni in his Technical Manifesto of Futurist Sculpture of 1912 called for the use of glass, wood, cardboard, cement, concrete, horsehair, leather, cloth, mirrors, and electric lights,[2]

Umberto Boccioni, *Unique Forms of Continuity in Space*, 1913, bronze (cast 1931), 43⅞″ × 34⅞″ × 15¾″. The Museum of Modern Art, New York. Acquired through the Lillie P. Bliss Bequest

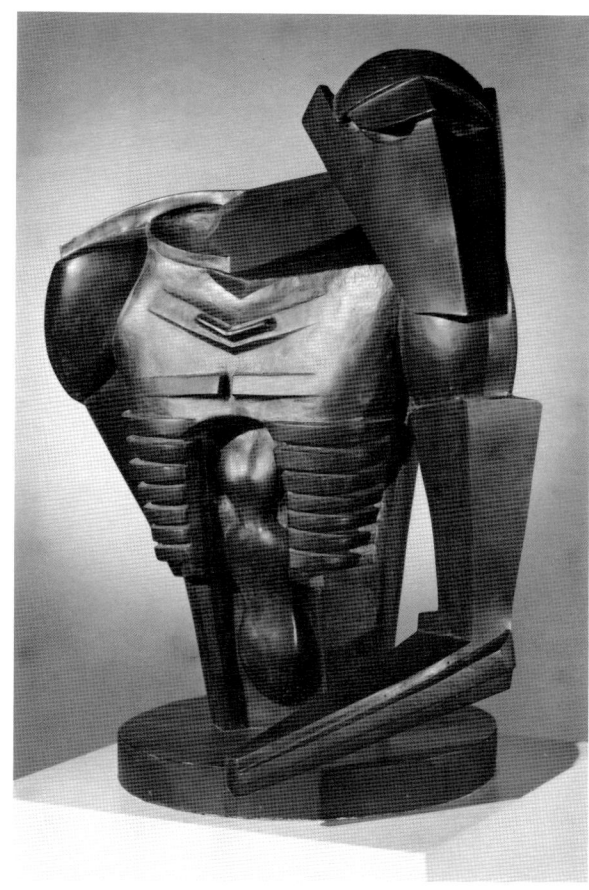

Sir Jacob Epstein, *Torso in Metal from 'The Rock Drill,'* 1913–14, bronze, 17½" × 27¾" × 23". The Tate Gallery, London

Marcel Duchamp, *Bicycle Wheel*, 1951, metal and wood, 50½" (H). The Sidney and Harriet Janis Collection, gift to The Museum of Modern Art, New York

in anticipation of the work some fifty years later of Robert Rauschenberg, Joseph Beuys, and Robert Morris. In the first version of Jacob Epstein's *The Rock Drill* (1913), the figure was positioned on an actual pneumatic drill, in a gesture that augured the tradition of assemblage and the incorportion into sculpture of actual objects. This sinister, robotlike creation stands as a sobering counterpart to the Futurists' enthusiastic heralding of the new Machine Age. However, the most shocking new sculptures of

this heady era were Marcel Duchamp's "ready-mades" or "found object" works. Selecting the most mundane, utilitarian, commercial items such as a *Bottle Rack* (1914) or a *Bicycle Wheel* (1913), Duchamp declared that their mere designation by the artist elevated them to the status of artworks. In mounting the bicycle wheel on a stool Duchamp mocked the idea of the base in sculpture, while the spinning wheel is an early precedent for kinetic sculpture.

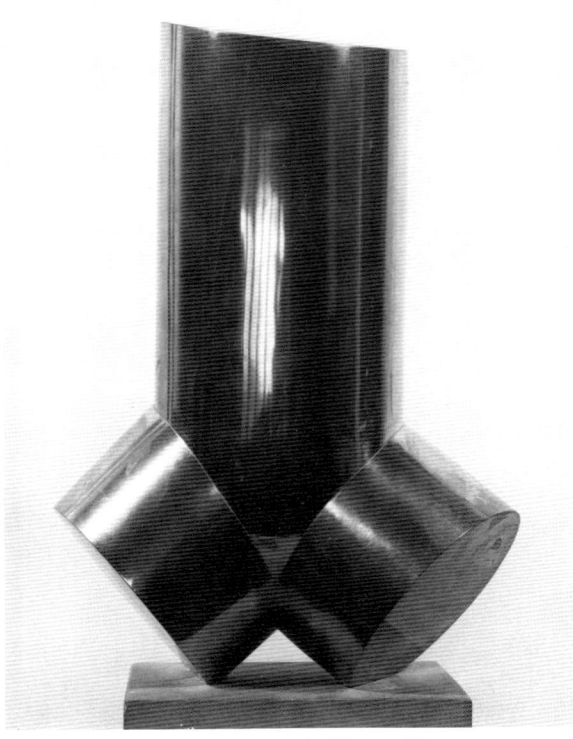

Constantin Brancusi, *Torso of a Young Man*, 1924, polished bronze, 18″ × 11″ × 7″.
Hirshhorn Museum and Sculpture Garden, Smithsonian Institution

Man (1917) likewise reduces its nominal subject to a schematic, highly polished bronze missile of three rounded cylinders. Rather than abandoning or using a neutral base, he actively incorporates the support as an integral part of the sculptural statement. The marble cube and carefully shaped hardwood support serve as textural, material, and formal counterpoints to the elevated bronze torso. Brancusi's three-dimensional, organic explorations were paralleled in the teens by Jean Arp's assembled, cut-out wood reliefs. His curved silhouette shapes, frequently painted in bright colors, were massed in overlapping planes and mounted on the wall.

In order to understand the achievements of post-Second World War, public, large-scale sculpture, it is essential to be familiar with the more intimate artistic experiments and discoveries of the movements described above. Yet it would be misleading to imply that no significant outdoor sculpture was produced during the late nineteenth century or first part of the twentieth. Rodin turned the direction of sculpture from the pervasive classical mode, but other sculptors persevered in an attempt to purify the classical idiom and extend the figurative tradition. Most prominently, Aristide Maillol created serene, bronze, life-size classical nudes almost invariably in repose. Maillol worked closely from the model in creating these unidealized outdoor works. Gaston Lachaise's recumbent females are more generalized earth goddesses. Though figurative and cast in bronze, the contrast of swelling thighs and bulging breasts with attenuated limbs, and the general floating appearance reveal the influence of biomorphism on the classical tradition. At the same time Jacques Lipchitz, a thoroughly Cubist sculptor, boldly created large-scale, public, abstract sculpture, such as *Song of the Vowels*.

Countering the pure, non-objective geometry of Constructivism and the analytical angularity of Cubism, the work of Brancusi heralds a third abstract tendency—biomorphism. The Rumanian-born Constantin Brancusi rejected realism as well as rectilinear geometry in favor of naturally rounded, smooth-surfaced, organically inspired, simple forms. His work is distinguished by a purity of concept, materials, and execution, characteristic of his reductivist aesthetic. In his hands the traditional portrait bust is reduced to a simple egglike oval of marble denied even a columnar neck, with only the slightest ridges to indicate features. His *Torso of a Young*

Perhaps the most decisive discovery that took public sculpture beyond bronze resulted from the experiments of Julio Gonzalez and Picasso in welding iron rods to create small-scale, linear sculptural pieces in the late 1920s and early 1930s. More than

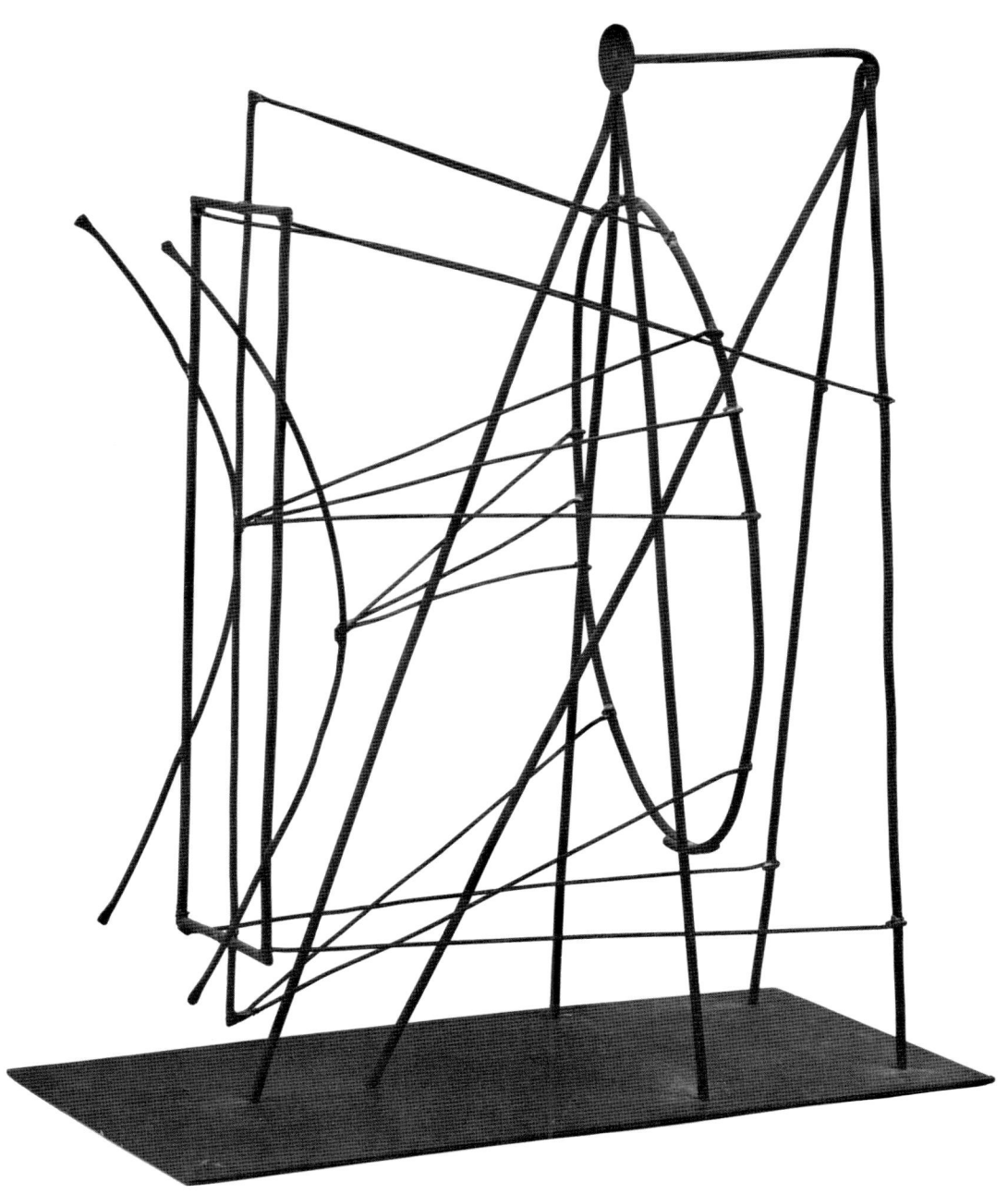

Pablo Picasso, *Construction in Wire*, 1928–29, metal wire, 19⅞″ × 16⅛″ × 7½″.
Musées Nationaux, Paris. Copyright, SPADEM, Paris/VAGA, New York 1981

Alexander Calder, *Lobster Trap and Fish Tail*, 1939, painted steel wire and sheet aluminum, 8′6″ × 9′6″. The Museum of Modern Art, New York

the form of their works, it was their material, their approach to assembling, and their process of welding that greatly expanded the vocabulary of modern outdoor sculpture by introducing a flexible medium that could withstand the elements. From that time the majority of large-scale sculpture would be assembled or formed from iron and steel, rather than cast in bronze or carved in stone.

The two artists who made the most significant contribution to the development of assembled metal sculpture were the Americans Alexander Calder and David Smith. Calder, the son and grandson of sculptors, moved to Paris in 1926, and was soon intimate with such Surrealists as Arp and Miró. Though also inspired by the Constructivists, Calder's early, austere, and open geometric constructions of wire and cutout metal, had a Surrealist quality of animation and whimsy. Calder's earliest works incorporated movement, activated by hand-cranking or electric motors. From the 1930s onward, his standing or suspended mobiles, as they were dubbed by Marcel Duchamp in 1932, were propelled by the wind. By the end of the thirties both mobiles and stabiles had increased dramatically in size and the strict geometric forms had given way to the freer, organic shapes in metal plate found in *Lobster Trap and Fish Tail* (1939).

From the early 1940s Calder revelled in the aesthetic possibilities afforded by the strength and durability of sheets of steel—cut, bolted together, and ribbed for strength. In all his works the strength of steel is exploited to permit openness and to conjure an illusion of lightness that belies their actual tonnage. Princeton's *Five Disks: One Empty* extends a vocabulary descended from such earlier Calder pieces as the nearly nine-foot-high sheet steel *Black Beast* of 1940. While basically a Constructivist work in the tradition of Pevsner's *Construction in the Third and Fourth Dimension*, *Five Disks* surrealistically transcends its own geometry to assume a decidedly zoomorphic guise, like a prehistoric creature perched on four legs.

While Calder pioneered large-scale sculpture by bolting steel, David Smith assembled with a welding torch. Smith, trained as a painter at the Art Students League, had learned to weld while working in a Studebaker plant in the summer of 1925. He first recognized the potential of open, welded sculpture in a reproduction of a Gonzalez piece in the art periodical *Cahiers d'Art*, and he applied this technique in his own work from 1933 onward. Throughout the thirties and forties Smith constructed small-scale, welded metal works that were linear in composition and Surrealist in mood. During the Second World War Smith worked in a locomotive factory and his subsequent sculpture increased dramatically in scale as he began to incorporate large machine parts in an abstract, Constructivist idiom.

In 1940 Smith established a veritable one-man sculpture factory in Bolton Landing, New York, naming it the Terminal Iron Works after his studio of the previous seven years in Brooklyn. Until his life was cut short by an automobile accident in 1965, Smith created an astounding range of large-scale work. Composing in a spontaneous, collagelike manner but with huge steel elements—both the found detritus of the Machine Age and carefully torch-cut elements—Smith was the artistic personification of the rugged, resourceful American pioneer.

Smith's background as a painter pervaded his sculptural thinking. In his low relief, collage manner of assembly he gave equal attention to shape as solid form or negative space and the majority of his work is two-sided rather than in the round. His sculptures were conceived as outdoor pieces, whose massed, geometric elements were intended to frame and to be read against the backdrop of the surrounding landscape. Moreover, the surfaces of these sculptures were frequently painted with gestural brushwork in the manner of Smith's Abstract Expressionist friends.

The sculptures on which Smith was at work at the time of his death were named *Cubis* in reference to their Cubist inspiration. In these pieces he limited himself to a formal vocabulary of the primary, geometric, two and three-dimensional forms of rectangle, square, cylinder, and circle. The anonymous neutrality of these classical forms was countered by the highly personal, almost playfully casual manner of their clustering and assemblage. Smith extensively worked the stainless steel with a circular metal grinding brush in sweeping, painterly strokes and the shimmering surfaces of these sculptures unpredictably reflect and capture the surrounding color and the ever changing play of sunlight and shadow.

Smith and Calder opened the way for large-scale, metal sculpture, Smith by incorporating machine parts and establishing the use of the welding torch for assembly, and Calder by utilizing motion and by working with steel fabricators. The next generation of sculptors actively pursued these new possibilities. For instance, Mark di Suvero assembles open structures that are virtually architectural in their heroic scale. Building with brute, raw materials—giant, discarded timbers, steel I-beams, rods, chains, and cables—he carefully balances these rugged elements in poised equilibrium. Frequently a counterbalancing element, suspended from the main structure, is free to move in stately pendulous arcs, when activated by strong winds or the spectator.

George Rickey has defined his intention to create "structures with movement."[3] His delicately balanced objects, activated by the slightest breeze, define space by their motion. A realization of the Constructivist ideal, the shimmering planes, sheer blades, and pivotal hardware articulate space through motion without recourse to mass. While Calder's pieces are playfully unpredictable, the complicated parabolic and elliptical spaces articulated by Rickey's structures are painstakingly predetermined. In addition to harnessing the wind, Rickey, like David Smith, burnishes his stainless steel surfaces to reflect the play of sunlight.

In the tradition of assemblage, the British sculptor Eduardo Paolozzi has welded together discarded machine parts to construct his works, and more recently has fabricated modular elements that are combined like shiny new machines. Louise Nevelson in the 1950s and 1960s assembled wall environments by stacking boxes filled with wooden objects discarded from demolition sites. These giant structures were painted black, white, or gold to unify the constituent elements. To make more permanent outdoor pieces in the late sixties, she worked with steel and utilized the services of the first large-scale sculpture fabricator, Lippincott, Inc. While Princeton's *Atmosphere and Environment X* is a carefully planned piece made up of various pre-cut modular elements, Nevelson also works more spontaneously at Lippincott, assembling three-dimensional works that combine rapidly cut, freehand forms with scraps culled from the shop floor.

Calder, Nevelson, and Paolozzi turned to metal fabricators to realize their pieces once the size of their conceptions outstripped the capacity of their studios. Large-scale metal fabrication requires a substantial amount of expensive heavy machinery. Certain individuals, like David Smith or more recently Isaac Witkin, have undertaken the role of latter-day Vulcans in learning the techniques, acquiring the equipment, hiring the assistants, and developing the muscle to fabricate the steel.

While most sculptors of large-scale works turned to industrial fabricators out of necessity, Tony Smith and other Minimal sculptors of the sixties actively embraced the aesthetic neutrality of industrially made art. Tony Smith, who began his career as an architect working with Frank Lloyd Wright, only turned to sculpture in the early 1960s. As an architect he was accustomed to having his designs realized by craftsmen and builders. The first Minimalist sculptor, he rejected color and personal touch in art, preferring classical rectilinear geometric forms and the anonymous appearance of industrial fabrication. Using various crystalline modules to generate shapes, he designed maquettes in cardboard for their eventual fabrication in steel. Princeton's *Moses* (1969–1970) reveals the richness and variety that can be achieved when the artist restricts himself to the barest means of a triangular module extrapolated in three dimensions. Clement Meadmore shares with Tony Smith a penchant for minimal geometric form, industrial fabrication, and anonymous monochrome surface. Rather than rectilinear crystalline structures, Meadmore's sculptures are dynamic curved extrusions. In *Upstart 2* (1970), the square section is extended and cantilevered in a vital, expressive manner that personalizes its geometric parts.

From the diminutive wire sculptures of Picasso and Gonzalez of the late twenties through the monumental, industrial designs of Tony Smith and Meadmore of the early seventies the unifying link seems to be the use of the welding torch. In this new sculptural tradition, works are assembled and constructed of sheet metal in an essentially additive manner, rather than the subtractive method of carving wood and stone or modelling and moulding for subsequent casting in bronze.

Yet typical of the diversity in twentieth-century sculpture, carving and modelling are essential to one of the most influential sculptors of our century, Henry Moore. Moore's primary inspiration comes from rounded natural forms rather than rectilinear geometry. His materials are wood, stone, and cast bronze and his organic sculptures are never far removed from human, animal, or landscape reference. His best known image is the large, regally recumbent, abstracted earth mother. These single, two- and three-part figures convey the timeless reassuring presence of slowly eroded landscape. They are exactingly modelled in three dimensions and characteristically fenestrated. Their surfaces are painstakingly textured and patined, leaving a precise record of the artist's hand. Princeton's *Oval with Points* is for Moore an unusually simple, almost symmetrical, abstract work. Apart from its dramatic size it is reminiscent of the organic forms of the Surrealist sculptor Jean Arp. Traditionally cast in bronze from the original plaster, it evokes shapes of stones worn by water and wind, or bone structure pressing outward beneath muscle and skin.

Noguchi and Pomodoro similarly extend the organic sensibility in handcrafted works of stone and bronze. Noguchi's exquisitely spare stone sculptures revel in the tactile appeal of highly worked and variegated surfaces. Like Brancusi he continually simplifies, refines, and reworks elementary forms without sacrificing their character to pure geometry. In addition to creating elegant sculptural objects he has designed complete sculptural environments such as the garden of the Beinecke Library, 1960–1964. While related to Japanese gardens these environmental works are antecedents for the site-specific sculptural projects of contemporary artists.

Arnaldo Pomodoro's highly polished bronze objects begin as minimal geometric forms. Their pristine surfaces are then opened up by the sculptor as if these shapes had been eroded by rust and decay. The interior revealed beneath the skin is an accumulation of machinelike parts resembling compacted detritus of space age technology. In this manner Pomodoro combines pure geometric form with the appearance of organic process, and creates the illusion of machine-made shapes re-formed by natural erosion. *Sphere VI* might be read as a metaphor for the sphere we inhabit or the decomposing remains of a spent satellite.

The most recent work on the Princeton campus, George Segal's *Abraham and Isaac* (1978) revitalizes the figurative tradition which largely has been eclipsed by abstraction in the twentieth century. Segal's reputation derives from his haunting, white plaster, life-size figures isolated within contemporary environs. Emerging first at the time of pop art, these figures were life casts made from human models and their settings were reconstructed with real objects. A typical Segal vignette, *The Gas Station* (1963) poignantly conveys a sense of alienation as a lone figure, surrounded by the fittings of any American gas station, sits passively on a bottle crate.

The theme of *Abraham and Isaac* was Segal's response to a commission commemorating the killing of students by National Guardsmen at Kent State University in May of 1970. While in the Old Testament story Abraham's hand was stayed, no such divine intervention occurred at Kent State. The nature

George Segal, *The Gas Station*, 1963, plastic and mixed media, 102″ × 288″ × 56″. The National Gallery of Canada, Ottawa

of the commission, choice of material (bronze), the biblical theme, and the depiction of the decisive narrative moment in the work reassert the continuing vitality of a centuries-old tradition of figurative sculpture. In addition to such specific details as the rope around Isaac's wrists and the manner in which Abraham's foot is propped on a small ledge of stone, Segal's theme of human sacrifice and the profound dignity of the protagonists recall Rodin's *Burghers of Calais*. In both works, the sculptors have been acutely conscious of the negative space surrounding and separating distinct figures. Yet while the burghers are disparately placed and distanced by solitary thought, Abraham and Isaac are psychologically bound and the space between them energized by the impending thrust of the knife.

During the past decade, art has increasingly reentered the public domain and moved outdoors from the cloistered realm of the museum. This welcome phenomenon is perhaps best explained as a convergence of public acceptance of modern art with the artists' inclination to work on a larger scale. Historically, two-and three-dimensional art works had always been integrated with public architecture. The tombs of Egypt, the temples of Greece and Rome, and the cathedrals of Europe reveal the rich legacy of this traditional marriage of art and architecture. Indeed in the post-Renaissance era through the nineteenth century one is hard pressed to find a public building, be it civic, ecclesiastical, or cultural, which is not embellished with murals or statuary. Similarly, free-standing statuary commemorating events and their protagonists, as for example the prototypical equestrian monument, populated city squares, parks, and major thoroughfares.

In our century, sculptors rejected this idealized form of memorial as the dictates of personal expression in art supplanted the expression of civic pride. The rejection of Rodin's *Balzac* was in retrospect a clear harbinger of the widening gap between public expectation and artistic expression. Moreover in the past fifty years the dominance of the International Style of architecture with its credo of "less is more" has largely purged buildings of any semblance of decoration or artistic embellishment.

At the beginning of the century avant-garde sculptors by and large withdrew from the public arena to pursue personal investigations and develop the implications of Cubism, Constructivism, and Surrealism on a more intimate and manageable scale. Since the end of the Second World War, confident in the validity of their new forms and following the lead of Calder, Moore, and David Smith, artists have responded by dramatically increasing the size of their sculptures. Intended for outdoor installation, sculpture once again tentatively entered the public domain at a time when a larger audience had become acclimated to the radical forms of modern art.

While at first only the most adventuresome university, city, or progressive corporation would acquire a large-scale work of sculpture, the success of these early experiments has led to a proliferation of public sculpture. This phenomenon is largely urban with sculpture initially being installed on the plazas that front the austere corporate and civic buildings throughout the country. Public art is perceived, and rightly so, as a successful means of humanizing the stark urban grid. Works of art enrich city life by reasserting human scale and lending particularity to anonymous spaces.

Large-scale sculpture is by no means restricted to urban settings. The advent of sculpture parks such as the Storm King Art Center in Mountainville, New York, provides a "museum of art" in a domesticated landscape. Increasingly colleges and universities like Princeton have integrated outdoor sculpture into their campuses. Yet the Putnam Memorial Collection is distinguished by its breadth, historic range, and the consistently high quality of the art works.

The John B. Putnam, Jr., Memorial Collection
Princeton University

1 Reg Butler
British, born 1913

The Bride

Bronze   Executed in 1961; installed in 1970
Signed and numbered on right foot: *RB 3*; inscribed on rear of base: *Cast by Morris Singer: Aslip*
Number 3 of edition of 8
Height: 7 feet 4 inches (2.35 meters)
Location: courtyard of Hamilton Hall

The felicitous choice of site for Reg Butler's *The Bride*—an intimate Gothic courtyard with fine trees —echoes the milieu in which the sculture was created. At his Elizabethan home in Berkhampsted, Hertfordshire, a house once occupied by Nell Gwynn, Butler has three workshops, which he refers to as his "three fields for cultivation."[1] One is a garden where *The Bride* evolved over a five-year period from an initial plaster that was repeatedly refined before final casting in 1961. "It was made entirely outdoors in a tree-surrounded garden," writes the sculptor. "Although I wouldn't claim a direct metaphor, *The Bride* probably owes a great deal to the adjacent tree trunks and the leaves around me all the time."[2]

The effect of this environment is apparent in the sculpture, for the figure seems to emerge, treelike, from the earth. The lower body simulates the clean contour of a tree trunk over whose textured surfaces light plays sensuously and variably. The armless torso swells into a crowning mass, which like foliage sacrifices definition of form to the mysteries of chiaroscuro. From the ambiguous volume of bridal veil, the allusive features of a woman's face emerge to reveal an introspective bride. Of *The Bride* and his method of working, Butler has written:

> I work to get things as "right" as I can, but what "right" means in any given instance I can only find out by making. I work on some figures over a very long period of time—for instance, 'The Bride' I started in 1956 . . . the studios are always full of sculptures some beginning, some ending, some soon to be abandoned others the early stages of things to be with me for years to come. I have

to work obliquely otherwise everything breaks up. One builds with the edges of one's vision.[3]

Born in Buntingford, Hertfordshire in 1913, Butler enjoyed the free encouragement of his parents to indulge a natural inclination for the arts. By the age of fifteen he was executing lively, if naive, paintings, sculptures, and prints. At twenty he embarked on a course of study to become an architect. Acquiring his license to practice in 1937, Butler became a successful consultant in industrial technology. But his insistence on devoting four days weekly to drawing and sculpture led inevitably, by 1950, to the logical decision to accept sculpture as his true profession.

The artist first achieved international recognition as the winner of the grand prize in a worldwide competition held during the years 1951–1953 for a memorial to commemorate the "unknown political prisoner." In the early 1950s the connotations of this tragic theme were still poignantly alive for much of twentieth-century society recently rocked by the horrors of World War II and its aftermath. For Butler, too, the competition had personal affinities. As a conscientious objector, he had long been convinced that another international struggle would annihilate the known social structure, and he had worked as a village blacksmith and repairman for local farmers in the belief that a disrupted world would have need of such basic skills after the war.

In Butler's prize-winning maquette,[4] which was destined never to be realized on a monumental scale, an elongated, skeletal tower stands open on a naked rock; three minuscule female figures, isolated on a lower rock, fruitlessly scan the empty tower and the limitless expanse of sky. Of this

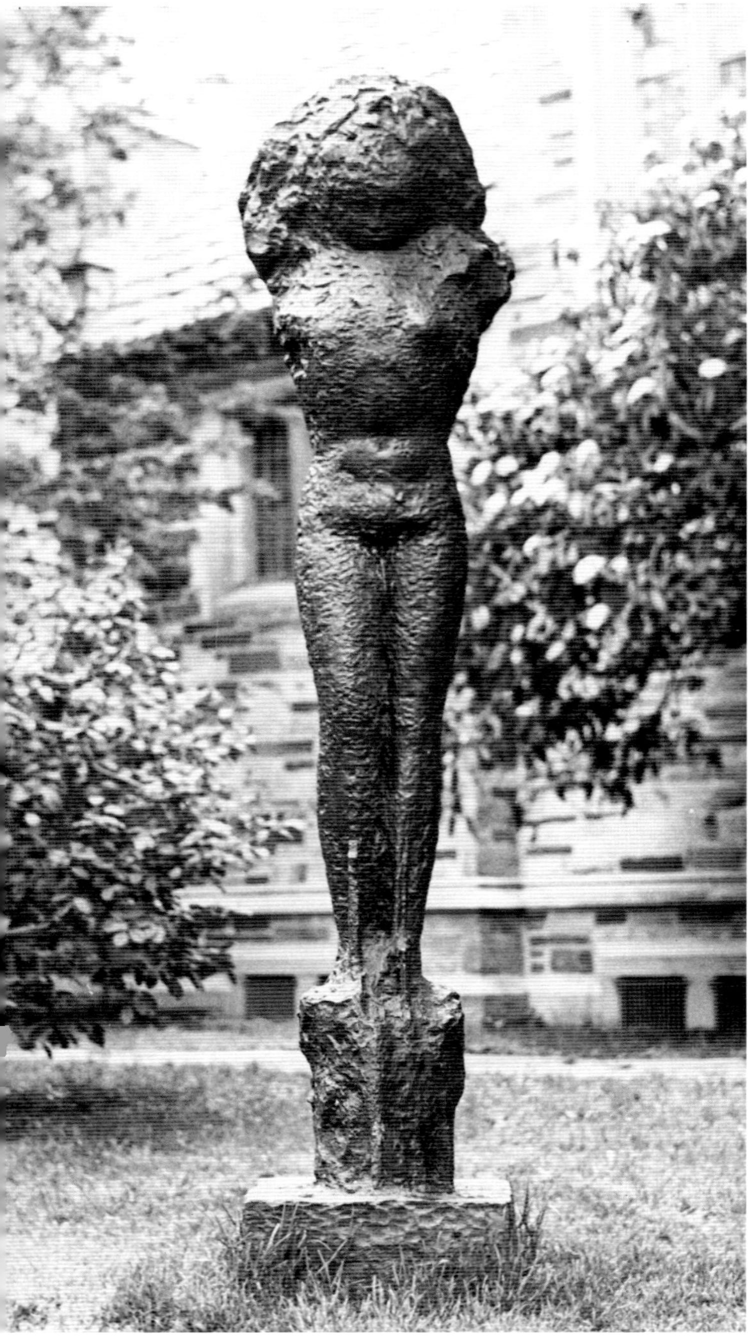

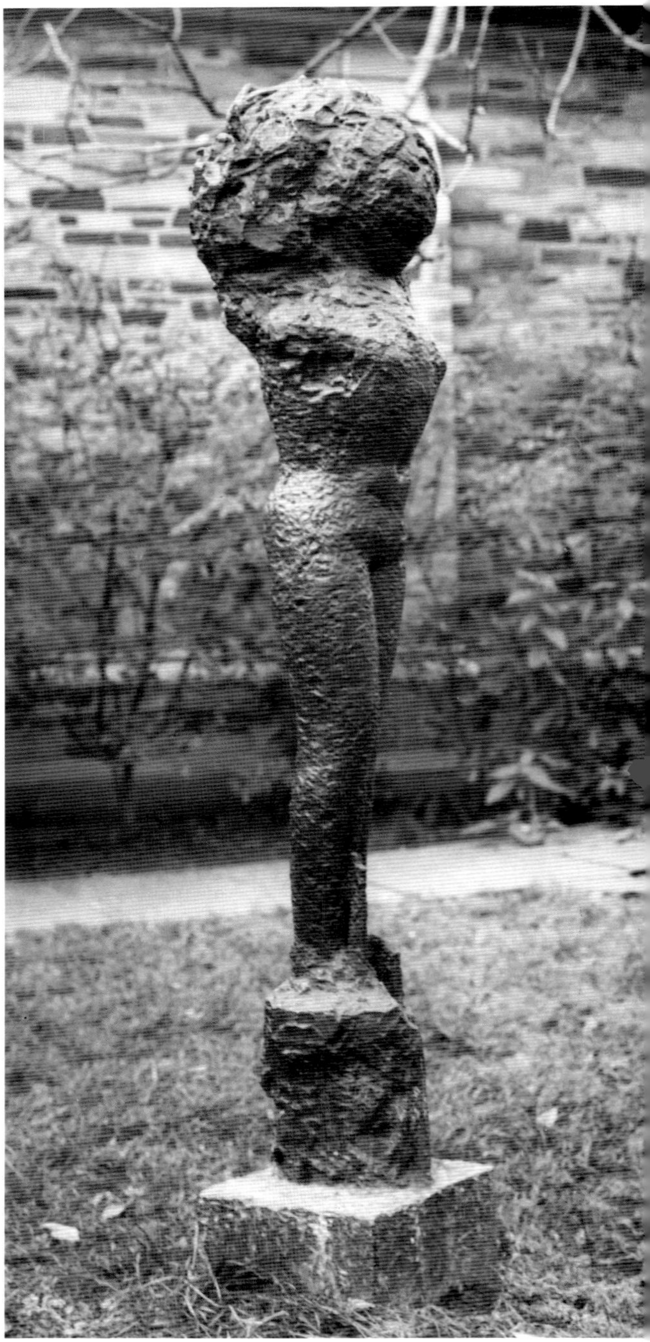

moving and harshly beautiful work, once suggested for erection overlooking West Berlin, an intuitive Robert Goldwater observed: "It is perhaps ironically fitting that this monument to unrecognized heroism was never built."[5]

Following the competition for the memorial, Butler entered into a rich and productive period in the fifties and sixties. From these years date some remarkable, single-figure sculptures (including *The Bride*), which are predominantly female forms caught in an act of arrested movement. These expertly revitalize traditional representational images, endow them with twentieth-century motivation and sensibility, and enable them to speak eloquently to a contemporary audience. In another group—termed "kite figures"—single human forms are seen suspended, falling, or hurtling through space. A third image was an enclosed boxlike volume elevated on stilts or a structural plinth. These enigmatic sculptures, called "tcheekles" by the artist,[6] were conceived as projects for monumental towers to inhabit extensive landscapes. In the late 1960s and early 1970s, Butler created a group of extraordinary, life-size representations of the female form in which bronze is colored in porcelainlike hues embodying qualities related to pop art and kitsch.

An instinctive experimenter and inventor, Butler has never been awed by either medium or technique in his work. As he has said: "I am convinced that the material is there to be used by me not to use me."[7] Drawing on his experience as a blacksmith during the war years, he was one of the first English sculptors to work in wrought iron in the later 1940s. After producing a number of abstract works in the vein of Gonzalez, he abandoned the medium in the early fifties to return to what he called "volume sculpture" and greater naturalism in style. To serve both practical and aesthetic needs in casting the figures of the next decade, Butler developed first the shell-bronze and then the aslip techniques. Discussing these, he writes:

> Shell-bronze aims primarily at likeness and is a workable craft technique. It involves depositing a thin metal coating against the mould from the inside to provide a more favorable reproduction, sculptural form in general, and the capture of the minute tensions that come from the artist's touch. Quite frankly, it was developed to enable us to cast our bronzes ourselves. Aslip is a different process but has the same aesthetic objectives. It introduced to foundry practice the refinement of processes formerly used only in the aircraft industry and involved the use of a sophisticated investment process. I developed it in an attempt to overcome the totally inflated cost of bronzes produced by bad casting techniques which demand endless patching, chasing and making good. Morris Singer, *fondeur* of *The Bride*, operated under licence to me for some time. Susse of Paris sent workmen to me to study the process but never acknowledged their use of the idea. As far as I know the method is no longer employed admittedly by anyone, but many aspects of the process, particularly the special waxes developed, are probably still in use by both Susse and Morris Singer.[8]

To date, four strikes of a proposed edition of eight have been cast of *The Bride*, each at a different time according to the artist. The Putnam version is numbered "3" on the sculpture itself.[9]

2 Alexander Calder
American, 1898–1976

Five Disks: One Empty
Mild steel, painted black   Executed in 1969–1970; installed in 1971
Signed and dated on foot: *AC* [artist's monogram] *70*
Height: 26 feet 3 inches (8 meters)
Location: plaza between Fine and Jadwin Halls

Calder's mobile sculpture is justifiably considered to be his single most important contribution to twentieth-century art: a legacy unparalleled for the multiplicity of images that erupted from a mind endowed with intuitive invention, a unique sense of fantasy, and an extensive knowledge of mechanical engineering. At the same time, Calder never lost interest in his stabiles.[1] New images, usually only a few feet high, appeared regularly in the decades between the early 1930s and his death in 1976. These sculptures were as imaginatively conceived, technically proficient, and innovative as their mobile counterparts. But what they needed was monumentality. Calder was aware that increased size did not necessarily enhance the aesthetic effectiveness of his mobiles, but he recognized that grandeur of proportion was an essential ingredient if his stabiles were to compete with other large-scale sculptures of the twentieth century. Fortunately, major international commissions arrived in the late 1950s that permitted the giant stabiles to be realized.

Works on such monumental scale, of course, could not be produced at Calder's studios in Roxbury, Connecticut, or Saché, near Tours in France. Nor could the task of fabrication be done by Calder alone. Seeking technical assistance, he settled on the Segre Iron Works in Waterbury, Connecticut, and later the Etablissement Biémont in Tours. These two firms were to realize most of Calder's sculptures in steel during the last decades of his career.[2]

In creating one of his giant stabiles, Calder first made preliminary sketches and then fashioned a small maquette in which his mental image was given its first three-dimensional form. Working with sheets of aluminum to assemble this prototype (normally about 20 inches high), the artist snipped, beat, filed, shaped, and finally riveted or bolted the various components into a design that satisfied him.

As a second stage, Calder called on his craftsmen to make an intermediate-scale model from the maquette, usually one-fifth of the dimensions of the finished sculpture. Employing this version for the study of technical problems of weight and balance, tension and stress, vibration and reinforcement, Calder regarded it as a working model of no aesthetic importance. Indeed, after many large commissions had been executed, and the sculptor and his technicians had acquired sufficient experience, Calder frequently eliminated this stage altogether. Such was the case in the creation of Princeton's *Five Disks: One Empty*, for which no intermediate model was required.[3] Once Biémont or Segre had the complete dossier of Calder's requirements, the full-scale work was fabricated in a provisional state and readied for the artist "to add the ribs and the gussets, or other things which I hadn't thought of. After that they work out my ideas on the bracing. And that does it."[4]

Negotiations for the acquisition of an important sculpture by Calder were initiated by the Selections Committee of the Putnam Memorial early in 1969. After showing interest in a medium-scale stabile then being exhibited in Europe, committee member Alfred H. Barr, Jr. approached Calder directly to discuss the feasibility of a more monumental work designed especially for Princeton. The sculptor responded that he was currently preoccupied, but that he would find it "fun to make something especially for you, and quite big . . . . So [I hope you will] bear with me, and I will evolve you something."[5] By early summer he was free enough to write: "I feel that now I can try to conjure something up for Princeton."[6]

The University's dual architectural complex of

Maquette, 1969, stapled aluminum cutout, painted black, 22½″ (H). The Art Museum, Princeton University. Gift of the artist in honor of Alfred H. Barr, Jr., Class of 1922

Construction at Etablissement Biémont, Tours

Fine Hall (mathematics) and Jadwin Hall (physics) was then nearing completion. Its slabstone plaza, grandiose in scale, was designed not only to establish a common relationship between two massive structures, but also to function as an avenue of access to nearby Palmer Stadium and to the central campus across Washington Road, the latter a primary artery into Princeton from U.S. Route 1 linking New York City and Philadelphia. This enormous mall demanded the central focus that a monumental sculpture could best supply. Calder had provided a comparable solution in his gigantic stabile *Teodalapio*, created in 1962 for Spoleto, Italy, which acts as a triumphal arch for traffic flowing into the town. With that as a precedent, site plans and photographs were sent from Princeton with the suggestion that Calder take into account the possibility of pedestrians and cyclists walking or riding through his sculpture. The artist responded with photographs and a maquette; the latter he subsequently presented to The Art Museum in honor of his longtime friend Alfred Barr. Following the unanimous concurrence of the Selections Committee and President Goheen, the process of construction was undertaken by Biémont in late 1969. At this point, Calder referred to the sculpture as "Disks and No Disks," and doubtless thought of its overall color as black.

Alfred Barr, however, temporarily seized by the contagion of Princeton nostalgia, recommended that one or more of the disks on the stabile be painted orange to honor the orange and black colors of Old Nassau. A wary Calder replied: "After overcoming

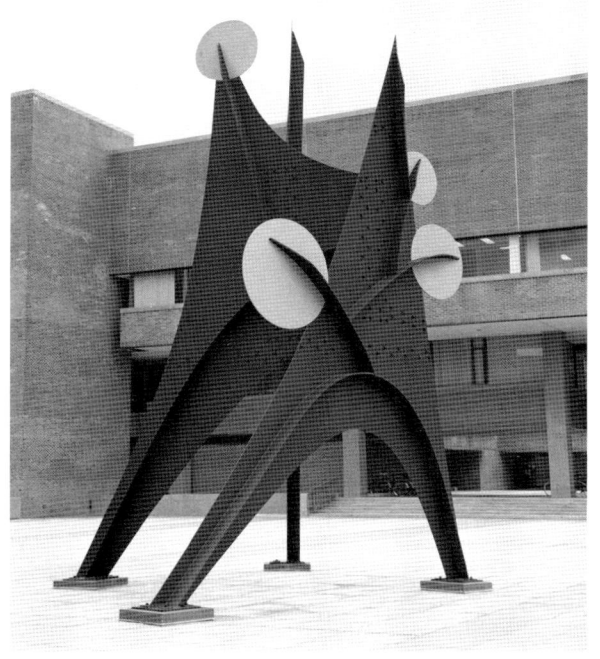

"Orange Disks"

my initial reluctance to paint anything orange, I think *all* 3 disks might be good."[7] A few weeks later he amended this: "I suggest that you paint the smallest '*Orange*.'"[8] Consequently, on its installation, the stabile variously bore the names "Many Disks: One Orange" or "Orange Disks," until the artist's visit to Princeton in November 1971. In anticipation of his arrival, all four solid disks had been painted orange, a hue that of course violated Calder's normal palette of primary colors. Surveying his sculpture with a shrewd, cocked eye, he shambled in and out of the stabile to scan the work from various angles of the plaza and from the top of the thirteen-story Fine Hall Tower. Then, he gave quiet instructions to the painters and the four orange disks were gradually blacked out, one by one. It was obvious that

Calder had made his point. To an inquiry about a new title for the stabile, he replied without hesitation: "Five Disks: One Empty." Clearly he had anticipated the denouement from the beginning.

Pleased with his accomplishment, Calder asked to visit the three lead sculptures—*Saint Michael, Saint George,* and *The Student Warrior* or *Fame* —executed by his father, A. Sterling Calder, in 1923 for the 1904 Henry and 1905 Foulke dormitories facing University Place. He would have enjoyed even more seeing the site of *Five Disks: One Empty* being used for senior proms, and participating with undergraduates as they danced under and about its elegant supports while colored lights played over its tall forms on nights in early June.

3 Sir Jacob Epstein
British, born in U.S.A., 1880–1959

Professor Albert Einstein
Bronze   Executed in 1933; acquired in 1970
Signed, indistinctly, on back: *Epstein*
Height: 16½ inches (.42 meters)
Location: Fine Hall Library

The American-born Jacob Epstein was a conspicuous contributor to the language of modern art in England in the first half of the twentieth century. Regarded during much of his lifetime as a bohemian *provocateur* of staid British sensibilities, Epstein had a directness of approach and an earthy naturalism that contrasted markedly with the elegant mannerisms of his older compatriots, Whistler and Sargent. He forged a double-edged personal style for himself while living and working in Paris between 1902 and 1905, influenced by Rodin in his portraiture, and later by Cubist-Futurist principles in his more ambitious exhibition pieces and public commissions. Epstein was also an unusually knowledgeable collector of sculpture from earlier Near Eastern and Mediterranean cultures, and from Africa and Indonesia—works whose stylistic vocabulary had not yet seeped into the general consciousness. When he endowed his own sculptures with something of the physical power and mystery of those archaic and primitive objects, he outraged critics and public alike, who saw his art as semi-barbaric, sometimes even blasphemous. Nonetheless, Epstein always attracted influential and wealthy patrons for his portrait busts and found powerful defenders for his controversial monuments. Eventually antipathy gave way to national pride; Epstein was knighted in 1954, and his later life was enriched by a number of nationally important commissions.

Certainly Epstein's ultimate reputation will rest largely on the galaxy of notable portraits he executed of celebrated personages from the Edwardian era until his death in 1959. A dazzling procession of intellectual and public figures sat for him, among them, George Bernard Shaw, Joseph Conrad, T.S. Eliot, Lady Gregory, Bertrand Russell, John Dewey, Paul Robeson, David Lloyd-George, Winston Churchill, Haile Selassie, Pandit Nehru, and Chaim Weizmann. Ranking among the best of these portraits, and with particular connotations for the Princeton community, is the bust of Professor Albert Einstein in the Putnam Memorial Collection.

In his autobiography, Epstein describes the execution of this portrait shortly after the celebrated scientist's flight to England from Belgium in 1933, following persistent rumors of possible assassination. The sculptor sought Einstein out at his drab and barren refugee camp at Cromer in Norfolk.

Einstein appeared dressed very comfortably in a pullover with his wild hair floating in the wind. His glance contained a mixture of the humane, the humorous, and the profound. This was a combination which delighted me. He resembled the aging Rembrandt....

I worked for two hours every morning, and at the first sitting the Professor was so surrounded with tobacco smoke from his pipe that I saw nothing. At the second sitting I asked him to smoke in the interval. Einstein's manner was full of charm and *bonhomie*. He enjoyed a joke....

Einstein watched my work with a kind of naïve wonder and seemed to sense that I was doing something good of him.

The sittings unfortunately had to come to a close, as Einstein was to go up to London to make a speech at the Albert Hall and then leave for America. I could have gone on with the work. It seemed to me a good start but, as so often happens, the work had to be stopped before I had carried it to completion.[1]

Einstein's *bonhomie*, his jokes, and sorties from

sittings to play a piano or scrape on an old violin,[2] led Epstein subtly to temper his portrait with faun-like touches—the suggestion of an animal earlobe and a persistent cowlick substituting for the classical attributes of the goat ears and horns of a playful Faunus.

Shortly after his arrival in the United States in 1933, Professor Einstein joined the faculty of the newly created Institute for Advanced Study in Princeton. During his long tenure there and his residence at 112 Mercer Street until his death in 1955, the world-famous physicist became something of a local legend in the Princeton community.

The Einstein bust was a popular one from the beginning, and knowledge of the definitive number of strikes made by Epstein is tenuous. It is generally believed that an edition of twelve was executed by the sculptor during his lifetime and we know from his autobiography that the first version was acquired for the Tate Gallery in London.[3] In any event, the original plaster was presented, together with some two hundred other models, to the Jerusalem Museum by the artist's widow in 1961 with the stipulation that no further casts ever be made. The Putnam Memorial bronze, from the collection of Mrs. Ida Yates, was acquired from Christie's, London, in October 1970.[4]

In addition to the Einstein portrait and two other fine busts by Epstein in The Art Museum collection, Princeton University also owns the original plaster head and torso of the Archangel Michael from the large-scale model of *Saint Michael and the Devil*, executed for the facade of Coventry Cathedral after its reconstruction following the bombings of World War II. This sculpture, one of Epstein's last master-works, was completed in 1958 and the finished bronze was dedicated at Coventry in 1960, after the sculptor's death. Princeton's imposing fragment, the gift of Lady Epstein to the University in 1965, is now permanently located in the south transept of the University Chapel. Like the Jerusalem models, it may not be recast.

In 1973 the Institute for Advanced Study in Princeton was bequeathed a cast of the Einstein bust by Joseph Schaffner, who had inherited the bust from his uncle, Hiram J. Halle. An American industrialist, Halle was both a personal friend and a financial supporter of Epstein in the early 1930s and the artist made a sculptured head of him in 1933, the year that Einstein also sat for his portrait. Halle's was one of the earliest strikes of the Einstein bust.[5]

Though the two versions in Princeton are identical in size and most other essential characteristics, the Institute bronze is unsigned, undoubtedly because of its early founding date; it has a dullish brown patina and depicts the distinctive forelock as lying rather close to the mass of unruly hair. The Putnam cast, on the other hand, is signed and has a rich green patina treated to endow the rough, free modeling with a tonal unity; the cowlick here becomes aggressively hornlike as a further complement to the fancied animal earlobe in the hair. These variations indicate that the sculptor, after he had filled the initial commissions for his popular bust, returned to the original plaster to make minor refinements at leisure, thereby enhancing his retrospective concept of the natural, irrepressible, and humane spirit that was Einstein.

4   Naum Gabo
American, born in Russia, 1890–1977

Spheric Theme
Stainless steel   Executed in 1973–1974; installed in 1974
Unsigned
Height: 8 feet (2.5 meters)
Location: courtyard of Engineering Quadrangle

Naum Gabo was an innovator of the first rank in an era notable for the number of major artists who, individually or collectively, altered man's capacities for visual experience and offered new and heightened perceptions of the many intangibles of twentieth-century existence. He was born Naum Pevsner in Russia in 1890, and studied medicine, then civil engineering, at the University of Munich. During the cataclysm of World War I and the revolution in Russia, Naum, joined by his older brother, the artist Antoine Pevsner,[1] found refuge in Norway. The name Gabo, with which he signed his first constructions in 1915, dates from this period. Together the brothers, with Gabo as the chief theoretician, began to evolve the concepts that had far-reaching effects on modern art when published in their *Realistic Manifesto* of 1920.

Gabo's highly perceptive intelligence was captivated by spatial relationships. Profiting from his training as an engineer and his knowledge of new theories of organic construction, he turned his attention to sculptural problems. Traditional sculpture had dealt with material bodies in terms of solid mass. In the past the artist's image, trapped in the stone, could be realized only by cutting away extraneous parts of the mass encompassing it. Even working with fashioned or molded material, the sculptor needed to fill space with the solid form of his object. Gabo, however, sought a new vision.

Using stereometry, an expeditious method for determining the measurements of volumes, Gabo employed a "stereometric cube" as his vehicle for research. This schematic design involved the removal of four of the six sides of a cube, retaining the top and bottom, and replacing the rejected planes with two internal, interlocking diagonals. Thus the illu-

sion of solid mass within the cube could be destroyed, allowing the interior space to appear open and free. In this way, Gabo released sculpture from reliance on mass and turned space itself into a sculptural element.

Of his productive Norwegian sojourn, Gabo said:

I was living in the fjords of Norway where the atmosphere was as if one were not of this world. Very often the sky was above and the sky was below and you felt as if you were between two skies. The sense of space was so intense that it helped me in my imagination to go on with that work, with my images, with the method of space.

That [stereometric] method left space open and by utilizing the free space you could give different aspects of the same image in the same volume of a sculpture. My conception took more than a whole year to realize in my sculpture, *Head*, finished in 1916. I have since made many sculptures based on that system.[2]

Returning to Russia after the revolution, Gabo and Pevsner became the motivating forces in the formulation of Constructivist ideas, which they proclaimed in a 1920 document written by Gabo and entitled *Realistic Manifesto*. This militant credo, posted on walls throughout Moscow and heralding a new era of artistic freedom, first stirred revolutionary Russia and then the world of art outside. Its innovative theories dealing with space, time, and motion in the arts, along with its practical espousal of such new materials as industrial metals, plastics, and glass, permanently enriched the language of twentieth-century art. The modern movement was initially approved by the Soviet government, which sponsored an exhibition of "New Russian Art" in

Berlin in 1922, with Gabo and Pevsner participating. But shortly thereafter, the party hierarchy labeled Constructivism and other innovative movements "of no service to the State."[3] The avant-garde was officially suppressed, and by late 1922 the Pevsner brothers and many fellow artists had left the Soviet Union. Gabo lived and worked successively in Berlin, Paris, and London for a quarter of a century before he settled in the United States in 1946, becoming a citizen in 1952.

Interspersed in Gabo's American years were notable lectures given at Yale, Princeton, and the National Gallery of Art in Washington; publication of his significant Mellon Lectures, *Of Divers Arts*; a visiting professorship at Harvard in the Graduate School of Architecture; and retrospective exhibitions in Berlin, Paris, London, and other European cities. There are major representations of his sculpture in the collections of The Museum of Modern Art, The Solomon R. Guggenheim Museum, Yale University, and numerous museums abroad. His masterwork for the Bijenkorf building in Rotterdam was completed in 1957 and his monumental fountain for St. Thomas's Hospital in London installed in 1976. In 1971 Queen Elizabeth II awarded Gabo an honorary knighthood in recognition of the close professional and personal ties he had long maintained with the artistic life of Great Britain.

Negotiations for the selection, commission, execution, and installation of Princeton's *Spheric Theme* extended over a four-year period. "It took a long time," said Gabo. "All these kinds of things always take time until they are materialized."[4] Time is indeed a significant element in the creation and in the ultimate experience of his work. The concept of *Spheric Theme* goes back to 1936, and has resulted in several variants. As Gabo explained in 1957:

> The *Spheric Theme* is the result of many years' research for a constructive method of transferring my perception of space in terms of visual experience of it. The angular structure of the stereometric cube which I applied in my previous constructions since 1915, I found in elementary stereometry. It very soon proved insufficient to many an image which was growing in me where the vision of space as a sculptural element had to play a greater role than in my previous images.
>
> I felt that the visual character of space is not angular; that to transfer the perception of space into sculptural terms, it has to be spheric. I was looking for some kind of an indication in the scientific world where a method of spheric structure could perhaps be found.
>
> I found no answer in graphic terms in science which would satisfy my vision of space. I consider that in this work of mine there is a satisfactory solution to that problem. Instead of indicating space by an angular intersection of planes, I enclose the space in one curved continuous surface. I eliminate angularity in space construction and give space the curved character which it has to my perception. I have used this system since 1936.
>
> I have made several variations on this theme in order to show its structural possibilities. There is an immense variety of images which a constructive sculptor may conceive which can be executed with the help of this system. There are some who consider my *Spheric Theme* as an image of infinity. To my mind the image of infinity could not be an image which turns back on itself. I feel in this *Spheric Theme* continuity rather than infinity.[5]

Versions of *Spheric Theme*, limited to a series of five to be executed by the sculptor, exist in the Edvard Munch Museum in Oslo, Norway; the National-Galerie, Berlin; the Mall, the New York State Capitol in Albany; and the Putnam Memorial Collection at Princeton University. The fifth version remained unexecuted at Gabo's death in August 1977.

5 Michael David Hall
American, born 1941

Mastodon VI
Bronze and aluminum   Executed in 1968; installed in 1969
Unsigned
Length: 87 inches (2.3 meters)
Location: entrance to MacMillan Building

Mastodon VI was acquired for the Putnam Memorial Collection from the 137 sculptures in the Annual Exhibition of Contemporary American Sculpture held at the Whitney Museum of American Art in 1968–1969.

Michael David Hall, then a twenty-seven-year-old assistant professor of art at the University of Kentucky, had shown publicly in New York City only once before, in "Sculpture in the Parks" earlier in 1968. He had to his credit, however, an impressive series of nine, large-scale, multi-media sculptures bearing the collective title *Mastodon*, a selection of which had been exhibited at the Vanderbilt University Gallery in Nashville, Tennessee during the previous March. Geometric in concept, these constructions consisted of judicious selections of materials as diverse as bronze, aluminum, steel, fiberglass, formica, and richly colored, acrylic lacquers, the latter "hand-mixed to avoid the non-colors of Detroit."[1] While certain contemporaries incorporated into their sculptures new elements mass-produced for industrial purposes or used "found objects" (discarded fragments of the Machine Age), Hall chose to cast his elements as independent forms and later to assemble them into his finished constructions. *Mastodon VI* is one such sculpture.

The *Mastodon* sculptures resulted from Hall's fascination with the primeval mystery of mammoth relics which he experienced during a 1963 job in search for fossilized mammal bones in the Badlands of Nebraska. "The smooth simple forms of the bones were sometimes fractured or cut by the wind and geologic action. They made stark silhouettes, emerging strongly and then often plunging right back into the flat crusty earth."[2]

Mastodon VI, with its tusklike tubular shapes in bronze erupting and flowing back simultaneously into verdant, lacquered hemispheres suggesting the earth, recreates Hall's experience with simple but opulent elegance. The obverse of the semidomes in polished aluminum creates further illusion through the fleeting reflections of nature that move in and out of its mirrorlike surface. Hall wrote of his work at the time of the Vanderbilt exhibition: "I consider myself a post-primary sculptor. What I am doing is parallel to, but separate from, minimal sculpture. My forms are by no means minimal nor are they necessarily 'pure.' Many of the conflicts and contradictions in my work are there by intention and are directed toward extending the impact of the image. I seek images which carry their own time and suggest their own mysteries."[3]

Since 1970, Michael Hall has been resident sculptor at the Cranbrook Academy of Art in Bloomfield Hills, Michigan. In recent years, his style has shown an increased affinity with Minimalism in its abandonment of multiple materials in a single composition and in the pristine simplicity of its conception. Constructions on a giant scale for the enrichment of public areas in both urban and natural settings have been Hall's major preoccupation. In 1973 he participated in an exemplary project entitled "Sculpture off the Pedestal," designed to enhance various public locations in the heart of Grand Rapids, Michigan with monumental abstract sculptures. Hall's 79-foot-long, painted wood construction *Sundance* was among thirteen works created *in situ* for this program.

The following year he collaborated in a similar project, "Sculpture in the Park," sponsored by the

Michael Hall, *Sundance*, 1973, painted wood,
16'5" × 79'4" × 19'. "Sculpture off the Pedestal,"
Civic Center, Grand Rapids, Michigan

Opposite: Michael Hall, *Cygnet*, 1974, painted steel,
5'11" × 120'7" × 11'8". "Sculpture in the Park,"
Grant Park, Chicago, Illinois

Auxiliary Board of the Art Institute of Chicago and
undertaken to exhibit in Grant Park, Chicago, five
contemporary monumental works that were too enormous and too heavy to be shown within museum
walls. Other participating artists were Mark di
Suvero, John Henry, Richard Hunt, and Kenneth
Snelson. Hall was represented with *Cygnet*, a low-
lying, 120-foot-long, painted steel construction.

Another mammoth, painted steel construction of
1974, entitled *El Tiburon*, was executed for the
campus of Wright State University in Dayton, Ohio.
Hall has described his vision of such works in contemporary society:

This type of sculpture is truly "outdoor" sculpture and traces its roots to the great structures of
pre-history such as Stonehenge.... My sense is
that the time is right for a work of this kind to
find its way into the environment of the American
academic community. In a time when so many
people are re-addressing themselves to questions
of relevance, I am certain that sculpture will give
new relevance to the notion that natural and man-
made environments can be intelligently and crea-
tively wedded to serve a broad range of human
intellectual and spiritual needs.[4]

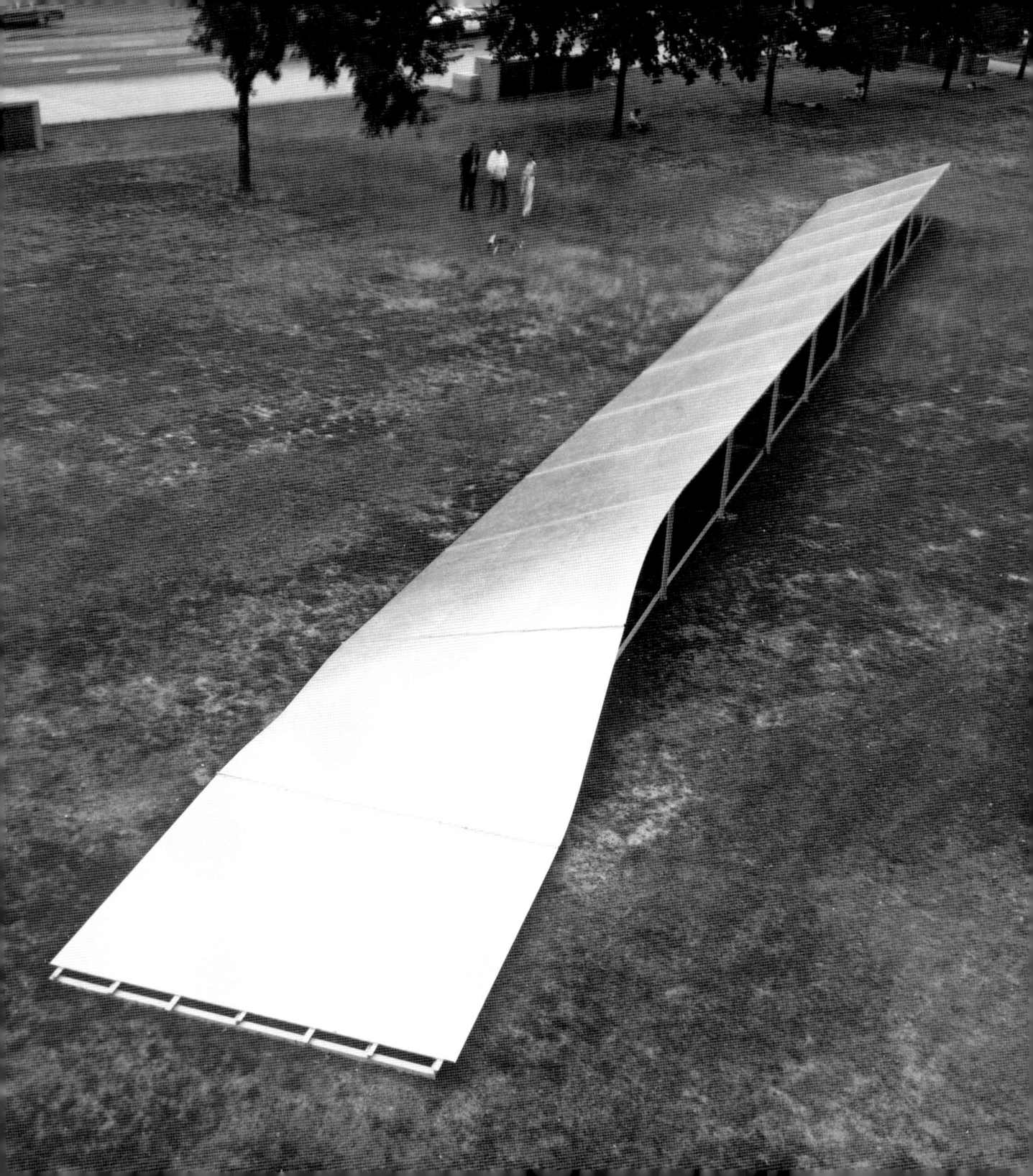

Gaston Lachaise
American, born in France, 1882–1935

Floating Figure

Bronze   Executed in 1927; installed in 1969
Stamped on left calf: *Lachaise Estate*, inscribed: 4/7; stamped on left foot: *Modern. Art. F.dry. N.Y.*
Number 4 of edition of 7
Height: 51¾ inches; length: 96 inches (2.5 × 1.3 meters)
Location: Compton Court, Graduate College

Despite the impact the Armory Show of 1913 had on a greening America, the acceptance of modern sculpture as a major art form came slowly in the next generation. Gaston Lachaise, with the support of a small but influential group of artists, critics, dealers, and intellectuals, was the chief protagonist in the struggle for its recognition in the period from 1915 to 1935, and emerged from the fray a figure of significant rank in American art.

The son of a cabinetmaker from the Auvergne, Lachaise was born in Paris in 1882. At thirteen he enrolled in the Ecole Bernard Palissey, a technical school for handicrafts and the arts, where the unusual abilities he displayed led to his acceptance by the Académie Nationale des Beaux-Arts in 1898 at the age of sixteen. For the next few years he worked casually at the academy, exhibiting yearly in the annual salons, competing for the Prix de Rome, and exploring and absorbing the luxury of experience that only turn-of-the-century Paris could offer.

Then, sometime between 1900 and 1905—it is said, while strolling in the Luxembourg Gardens—he met Isabel Dutaud Nagle, a Canadian-American from Boston, who was living apart from her husband. Lachaise's subsequent life—and art—are unimaginable without the presence of this woman and the visual image he created of her. Leaving the Beaux-Arts, he took a job with the Art Nouveau jeweler and glassmaker René Lalique for a year to accumulate enough money to pursue Mrs. Nagle to Boston. Though she refused to consider divorce and remarriage until 1913 when her son had entered Harvard, Isabel had become long since for Lachaise a Galatea, model, wife, and eternal mistress.

When Lachaise arrived in Boston in 1906, with thirty dollars and no English, sculpture in America was generally considered an art secondary to painting. Deemed a medium chiefly appropriate for war memorials, pseudo-classical allegories, or portraits, its commissions were generally awarded by committees selected from the academies, beaux-arts societies, or the political arena. Lachaise's first job in the New World was as an assistant to Henry Hudson Kitson, of Quincy, Massachusetts, who was then executing his Civil War memorial commemorating the Confederate dead at Vicksburg. Lachaise's precision training with Lalique proved invaluable to Kitson in the execution of details of military costume and weapons. Though the younger man thought Kitson's work contemptible, he followed him to New York in 1912 as an assistant, but soon established his own studio and began his first masterwork, *Standing Woman*, later termed *Elevation*. The following year he exhibited a small clay figure in the Armory Show, became an assistant to the modish sculptor, Paul Manship, and married Isabel Nagle.

By 1918, despite time-consuming work for the popular Manship, Lachaise was ready to hold his first one-man exhibition at the Stephen Bourgeois Gallery; the twenty-nine works, most of moderate or modest scale, included the life-size treated plaster of his *Standing Woman*. Though the work was generally well received, Daniel Chester French, then a high priest of orthodox sculpture, "shaking with rage and shock," castigated Bourgeois: "His vision is monstrous, how can you show these things?"[1]

Lachaise now became associated with many of the leading avant-garde artists and intellectuals of

the day. He was featured often in *Dial Magazine*, a monthly dedicated to the best new directions in contemporary thought and the arts, and the farsighted collector of modern art, A. E. Gallatin, made him the subject of a monograph with photographs of his sculptures by Charles Sheeler (1924). He executed some exceptional portrait busts, including those of John Marin, Alfred Stieglitz, Georgia O'Keeffe, Marianne Moore, e.e. cummings, George L. K. Morris, and Lincoln Kirstein. Exhibiting with Stieglitz in 1927, Lachaise began to receive important commissions, such as those for the RCA and International buildings in the Rockefeller Center, New York, and the World's Fair Exhibition in Chicago.

Executed in plaster in 1927, *Floating Figure* was first shown in 1928 at the Brummer Gallery,[2] New York, in an exhibition of twenty-eight works by Lachaise which included *Elevation (Standing Woman)* of 1912–1927, now cast in bronze. Gerald Nordland has described *Floating Figure* as:

> . . . rising in the air, balanced with an exuberance, lightness, and originality for which even the *Elevation* could not prepare one. The proliferation of rounded breast and buttock shapes creates a fantasy of sexually laden forms which communicate in the most forceful manner, while transfigured in the myth-making process into an extraworldly spirit . . . . Lachaise has etherealized his earth mother, provided her with the energies of all the gods . . . . As one sees the figure, one has no sense of weight or mass but only the qualities of serenity, strength and exalted womanhood.[3]

The year 1935 proved to be both fruitful and fateful for the sculptor. Granted an important commission to execute a "Memorial to the Peoples of America" for Fairmount Park in Philadelphia, Lachaise was given a major retrospective exhibition of his work early in the year at The Museum of Modern Art, that vigorous and youthful champion of contemporary style. At the exhibition, *Floating Figure* was first seen cast in bronze.[4] This strike was later given to the museum "anonymously, in memory of the artist," and has long been a glory of the museum's sculpture garden. In October 1935, at the age of fifty-three, after a sudden and unexpected four-day illness, Lachaise was dead. Isabel survived another twenty-two years until 1957.

Most of the sculptor's work, largely uncast during his lifetime, passed on his widow's death to the Lachaise Foundation, which places strict limitations on the number of casts authorized. Strikes, such as the one at Princeton, bear the designation "Lachaise Estate" and their number in the series of foundation castings, excluding any strikes that existed before its activities began. *Floating Figure* is limited to a total edition of eight, of which The Museum of Modern Art's bronze, struck in 1935 under the artist's supervision, constitutes the first. Subsequent foundation casts, all executed at the Modern Art Foundry in Long Island City, are numbered and located as follows: 1/7, Society Hill, Philadelphia; 2/7, Stark Collection, Los Angeles; 3/7, Sheldon Memorial Art Gallery, University of Nebraska, Lincoln; 5/7 The Australian National Gallery, Canberra; 4/7, Putnam Memorial Collection, Princeton University.[5]

7   Jacques Lipchitz
American, born in Lithuania, 1891–1973

Song of the Vowels
Bronze   Executed in 1969; installed in 1969
Inscribed on top of base: *7/7 J. Lipchitz 1931–32, Modern Art Foundry* (indistinctly)
Number 7 of edition of 7
Height: 10 feet (3.1 meters)
Location: between Firestone Library and the Chapel

Lithuanian by birth, Lipchitz was modeling at the age of thirteen. Though his father sought to turn his interest to engineering, his mother sent him to Paris when he was eighteen to study sculpture at the Ecole des Beaux-Arts and the Académie Julian. In Paris, through his friendship with Diego Rivera, he was introduced into a circle that included Modigliani, Soutine, Max Jacob, and Gertrude Stein. He was brought as well into the orbit of the Cubists—Picasso, Braque, and Juan Gris. One of the first artists to explore Cubist canons of form in three-dimensional media, Lipchitz became the foremost Cubist sculptor. Though his later work expanded beyond the formal restrictions of the style, the artist continued to insist that he was "always a Cubist"—and indeed he was, in the persistent sensitivity to formal relationships that he brought to his sculpture.

By 1927, Lipchitz had evolved in his "transparencies" one of his major contributions to modern art. These small-scale, modeled sculptures preserved the solidarity of form and structured design of the Cubist tradition but introduced open spaces that pierced masses to create voids that were as expressive as solids. The original clay maquette for *Song of the Vowels* in The Museum of Modern Art exhibits the concept of the "transparency" applied to a design for a monumental sculpture. This small masterpiece, characterized by élan and seemingly effortless vitality, is a very personal autograph of the artist. A master modeler, Lipchitz used his fingers as tools, and frequently signed major works not only with his name but also with his thumbprint.

Lipchitz executed the initial large-scale *Song of the Vowels* during the years 1931–1932 for the garden of the villa of Mme Hélène de Mandrot at

Le Pradet (Var) in the Maures mountains. After her death, this first strike was moved to the Kunsthaus in Zurich. Prior to 1969, when the last of seven casts authorized and personally executed by the artist was struck for the Putnam Memorial, five other variants had been made by the sculptor.[1] The variations result from the sculptor's reworking of his original concept in each successive bronze. Princeton's version, for example, adds a square plinth to the columnar pedestal of the sculpture proper— an element not found in earlier casts.[2]

Song of the Vowels is one of a succession of sculptures produced over almost two decades—the others are *The Harp Player* (1928), *Harp Players* (or *Harpists*) (1930), and *Benediction* (1945)—in which Lipchitz explored his "obsession" with the motif of the harp, inspired originally by the harpists at symphony concerts in Paris: "Invariably—the music contributing—the peculiar shapes of the harps, their strings vibrating in the light, veritable columns binding earth, transported me into a world from which I, in turn, had to make my way back under pain of losing myself there. From these repeated journeys was born, in the beginning of 1928 ... *The Harp Player* ... a sculpture made entirely of cords—a 'transparent' sculpture which can be seen and affects us from all sides at once."[3]

In *Song of the Vowels* harp and harpist are synthesized in an outburst of common exuberance. Cubist principles of structure and form are fully realized. The vision of "transparency," produces spatial tensions through open penetrations that puncture the blocklike mass of bronze to create a sense of lightness and a soaring elegance. As A.M. Hammacher has observed, "the harp gains the strength of wings."[4]

Of the poetic title of the sculpture, Lipchitz commented in 1946: "The title had no connection with the famous poem of Rimbaud, but rather with a legend of ancient Egypt, according to which it appears there existed a prayer, the *Song of the Vowels,* which the priests and priestesses made use of to conjure up the forces of nature. And it is to this capability of man that I have consecrated my work."[5] Lipchitz referred to this theme, though in slightly different words, on two other occasions, In 1965 he wrote to Dorothy C. Miller of The Museum of Modern Art: "Yes, *Song of the Vowels* has a symbolic significance. It has to do with a papyrus which relates to a song which existed in old Egypt. The song was sung to subdue the forces of nature and called the 'Song of the Vowels.' And to this power of the human being I dedicated my sculpture."[6]

And in 1972, in the autobiographical *My Life in Sculpture*, he reiterated: "I decided to attempt a monument suggesting the power of man over nature. I had read somewhere about a papyrus discovered in Egypt having to do with a prayer called the 'Song of the Vowels,' a prayer that was a song composed only of vowels and designed to subdue forces of nature."[7]

Discrepancy in these accounts—the naming first of "a legend of ancient Egypt" and then of "a papyrus" as the inspiration of the title and of his sculpture—indicates only a cursory concern by Lipchitz for his source, whatever this may have been. Of greater significance is the reiteration, in all accounts, of his dedication of the sculpture to man's capacity to evoke and to deal triumphantly with the forces of nature. Lipchitz typically recast traditional iconography to suit modern needs; his *Prometheus Strangling the Vulture, Theseus and the Minotaur, Return of the Prodigal*, and other works are familiar milestones of twentieth-century art. For him the connotation behind the myth was an eternal truth. The

Jacques Lipchitz, *Prometheus Strangling the Vulture* (reduced version), 1937, no. 1/7, 36″ (H).
The Art Museum, Princeton University. Gift of Cornelia McNamara in honor of the Class of 1929

hybrid harpists of *Song of the Vowels* equate solids and voids, consonants and vowels, and reveal the artist's unshaken belief in man's capacity to be gloriously triumphant, like the biblical David, through music and song.

Lipchitz first came to the United States in 1941. After World War II and a brief sojourn of a year in Paris, he returned to New York and eventually became an American citizen in 1958. In his celebrated studios at Hastings-on-Hudson and at Pietrasanta in Italy he continued to exert his extraordinary creative energy and vitality until his death in Capri in 1973 at the age of eighty-one. He was buried in Jerusalem.

Maquette, 1931, terracotta, 14½″ (H).
The Museum of Modern Art. Gift of the artist

8 Clement Meadmore
American, born in Australia, 1929

Upstart 2
Painted Cor-Ten steel   Executed in 1970; installed in 1973
Unsigned
Number 1 of edition of 2
Height: 21 feet
Location: entrance to Engineering Quadrangle

The Minimalist movement is characterized, in Hilton Kramer's words, by the impulse to reduce the language of art to "its sparest and barest elements. . . . to secure a maximum of expression at the very boundary separating art from nonart. There has always been an immense gamble at the heart of this impulse—the chance that the boundary would be crossed," leaving the work of art to be "lost either to decoration or to mere 'ideas,'"[1] *Upstart 2* is a sculpture ingeniously realized as a result of Meadmore's "immense gamble" to achieve purity of image through strict economy of means.

The image projected instantly creates a precise optical experience. An elongated, square-section tube of steel appears to twist from one extremity into a steadily rising curve that approximates a skewed circle. From the point of imminent conjunction, the remaining section of the tube abruptly shifts direction to shoot boldly skyward like an inclined monolithic shaft. Although it is constructed of two immense components joined together, the visual impression is of a single continuous form. Despite its actual mass and weight, the sculpture creates a miraculous impression of material lightness in the sinuous flow of form and surface. Its displacement of space carries additional impact from the aggressive way in which it seems to elbow out the surrounding atmosphere as it makes its ascent. In human terms, *Upstart 2* suggests a personality that is youthful, self-possessed, and bumptious—all attributes not commonly associated with monumental sculpture. It is said that "Meadmore sees his sculpture as being like a person who inhabits a place."[2]

The artist's means of achieving much with little in his sculpture first involves the execution of a small-scale maquette usually made of polyurethane. When completed, this model appears to have been formed simply from an attentuated bar that has been twisted, bent, stretched, curved, coiled, or knotted according to the sculptor's whim. It is, however, the result of considerable preliminary experimentation. Of his procedure, Meadmore writes: "My sculptures are all made on a trial and error system using small cast quarter-circle segments derived from the rotation of a diagonally positioned square around an external axis, and resulting in a series of conically curved surfaces which, in a few combinations, manage to transcend their geometric origins."[3] Once completed, the maquette is delivered for fabrication in Cor-Ten steel to Lippincott, Inc., in North Haven, Connecticut, a firm whose craftsmen specialize in the execution of monumental sculptures in concrete or steel for many of the major artists of our time.

Trained as an engineer and industrial designer before turning to sculpture, Meadmore exhibited widely in his native Australia before he moved to New York in 1963. He was among the first sculptors to recognize the potential of Cor-Ten. Since first obtaining the material from U.S. Steel in 1963,[4] he has employed it almost exclusively for his larger sculptures, attracted by its non-reflecting surface and its hardness and durability as a medium outdoors.

Because Cor-Ten has become such a popular material for contemporary sculptors since the early 1960s, a note about its basic attributes is in order. A particularly thick, hard steel, Cor-Ten is silver-gray when it emerges from the foundry. The raw metal is then sandblasted to produce a pitted surface comparable to coarse-grained sandpaper. Pocks created by the sandblaster act as a binder during the course of the oxidized rusting that ensues; gradually this forms a rich, dark brown patina as the metal weathers.

Maquette, 1970, black plastic, 7¾″ (H).
The Art Museum, Princeton University. Gift of the artist

The result is a warm, opaque texture, like the weathering encountered in found objects that has appealed to so many twentieth-century artists. Unfortunately, as in all rust formations, the surface of Cor-Ten tends to be delicate and care must be taken not to interfere with its overall consistency. When patch damage occurs, only a second, total sandblasting can achieve once again a uniform encrustation duplicating the original surface.

The strong and personal character of Meadmore's sculpture derives from his uncanny ability to endow three-dimensional forms with Minimal pictorial components. But where Meadmore differs from Minimal theory is his rejection of fixed relationships between elements of a composition in favor of fluid lines, edges, and surfaces that give his sculptural forms a pictorial quality. As he says: "My aim is always the same—to use geometric form in such a way as to achieve the expressive range normally associated with modelling, thus gaining the advantages of both."[5]

According to Meadmore, "*Upstart* 2 is the second of a series of vertical pieces which I work on infrequently because most of my pieces seem to end up being horizontal."[6] From the miniature working model, later presented by the artist to Princeton, he first executed a reduced version, measuring 25½ inches high, in an edition of four strikes. Completed in 1970 and cast by Lippincott, Inc., the enlarged version at Princeton is the first of an authorized edition of two sculptures on monumental scale; its replica has not been executed to date. In 1972 it was erected on its present site, in front of the School of Engineering, under the personal supervision of the sculptor.

By 1976 Meadmore had turned away from his earlier recurrent motif of a single, elongated bar molded imaginatively into a wide range of contorted sculptural images.[7] More recently, multi-part elements have constituted his constructions, although his language of style remains constant. Retained as ingredients are the square-section tube (now become multiple and truncated), the lively curved shapes (now fragmented), and the light-absorbent surfaces. As before Cor-Ten, painted matte black or allowed to form a natural encrusted rust, remains the preferred medium.

Clement Meadmore is represented in the collections of most major museums in Australia; the art institutes of Chicago and Portland, Oregon; Columbia, Princeton, and Houston universities; the New York State Capitol at Albany and the City of New Orleans; The Nelson A. Rockefeller Estate, Pocantico Hills, New York Collection; Chase Manhattan Bank, and numerous corporate collections. In 1968 Meadmore was among eighteen artists chosen to create sculptures for the Olympic Games held in Mexico City, and subsequently he has executed a number of major works for exhibition in civic and state-sponsored projects throughout the United States. In 1973, the artist was honored with a "Citation for Sculpture" by the National Academy of Arts and Letters.

9 Sir Henry Moore

British, born 1898

Oval with Points

Bronze   Executed in 1969–1970; installed in 1971
Unsigned
Number 1 of edition of 6
Height: 11 feet (3.3 meters)
Location: between Stanhope Hall and West College

At the time the gift of funds to create the Putnam Memorial Collection was made to Princeton in 1968, the anonymous donor also proposed a list of "masters of modern sculpture" considered "potentially suitable for purchase." Only one name appeared in the first category, that of Henry Moore. It was a choice consistent with contemporary opinion. Equalled only perhaps by Alexander Calder, Moore has been the sculptor most sought after in our day by architects, urban planners, landscape designers, and public, corporate, and private collectors, as a creator of monumental works to enhance outdoor spaces.

From its initial meeting in March 1968, the Selections Committee gave priority to the search for a major bronze by the British artist. Fortuitously, Moore was coming to the United States in mid-May of the same year to receive an honorary degree from Columbia University, and he was invited to visit Princeton. After a profitable exchange of ideas, it was agreed to drop consideration of two recent sculptures as inappropriate to the collection, and to await the development of others that Moore was working on at the time.

By March 1969, the first choice of three new sculptures, all in various preliminary stages, was offered to the University. *Oval with Points*, then in maquette form, was selected by unanimous decision of the committee, and President Goheen authorized the commission for its execution shortly thereafter. Concurrently, the artist decided to cast the 5½-inch-high maquette (reserved for his own collection) in an edition of nine miniature bronzes. Harry A. Brooks, Class of 1935, acted to reserve one strike for Princeton and, together with Wildenstein and

Co., Inc., presented it to the University for the Putnam Memorial Collection of artists' maquettes.

Moore's maquettes often reveal the creative process involved in the execution of a major sculpture more graphically than do those of artists who choose to work in steel or other less pliable materials. His *bozzetti*, created in plaster and in harmony with the sculptor's touch, are susceptible to manipulation at any stage of development prior to final casting. If the initial working of a model turns out to match Moore's projected concept, it is then turned over to assistants for enlargement in plaster, under his supervision, to any desired size. In correspondence dealing with *Oval with Points*, he wrote of this procedure: "The maquette is too small for me to work out the armature for the large full-size one, so I have nearly finished a working model which will be about 3 ft. 6 inches high; otherwise the jump from the little one to the very large one could give trouble."[1]

It is common practice for artists to alter their ideas during the execution of a work of art. This process is apparent in a comparison of Moore's miniature bronze, cast from the original maquette, with the monumental version. Most striking is the change in the relationship of the two points of the oval. In the small bronze these appear stubby and blunt, and the congress between them is diffident and tentative. In the final resolution, the points have become elongated and aggressively sharp, almost touching one another. One senses a tension between them, as between the fingers of God and Adam in Michelangelo's fresco of the creation of Adam in the Sistine Chapel.

Since Moore had his original maquette cast in bronze at an early stage, he presumably considered

Maquette, 1969, bronze, 5½″ (H). The Art Museum,
Princeton University. Gift of Harry A. Brooks,
Class of 1935, and Wildenstein and Co., Inc.

the design finished and ready for enlargement preparatory to final casting. But somewhere in between, his concept of the expressive value of the points changed, probably during the execution of the intermediate working model he described. Other modifications can be seen in the slight upward attenuation of the piece as a whole, the amelioration of the lumpy protuberances of the oval, and the general sharpening of some defining edges.

Two years after *Oval with Points* was commissioned, the completed 2½-ton sculpture, cast in England by the Morris Singer Foundry and patined by Moore himself, was delivered and installed. It became an almost immediate success on the campus. Both the Princeton community and visitors were attracted to the womblike form through its tactile appeal and its open invitation of empathetic security. Within a few short months—to the delectation of the sculptor —the interior curves of the oval had been burnished through contact with bodies sitting on or sliding through it. Like far older landmarks of Princeton, *Oval with Points* soon seemed to have been always there, rooted between Stanhope and West College and flanking Nassau Hall.

Since his student days, Henry Moore has had a strong attachment for stones, bones, shells, driftwood, and other natural objects.[2] His special fondness for one skeletal found object in particular has intriguing connotations for the origin of *Oval with Points*. The object, an elephant skull, had been acquired in East Africa by the distinguished scientist Sir Julian Huxley and his wife Juliette, and placed in their English garden, "where for three years it presided, its bony structure architectural in quality, still exud-

ing the giant creature's past vitality .... The skull, like the animal itself, was constructed on a vast scale—we could reach our arms up to the elbow in the empty sockets of its tusks."[3] Sensing the fascination that its "strange brooding presence" had for their friend Moore, the Huxleys gave him the skull: "Henry not only took it to his heart but proceeded to explore its massive outline, its tunnels and cavities, its recesses and blind eye-sockets, and to etch every aspect of its complex lineaments.[4] ... [He] also created several pieces of sculpture bearing the unmistakable stamp of his genius fused with an evocation of the skull's construction."

One of the sculptures Huxley speaks of was assuredly *Oval with Points*. On a visit in 1969 to the artist's home and studio at Perry Green, Much Hadham, Hertfordshire, to see the intermediate plaster model for the Putnam commission, the author was also shown the elephant skull. Though Moore himself did not refer to a connection between his model for the sculpture and the mammoth cranium, definite affinities could be discovered between the general form of *Oval with Points* and the subtle undulant surfaces of the skull bones as well as suggestive shape of the optical cage long since devoid of eyes.

The Putnam sculpture is unique in the United States. Since it was installed in the spring of 1971, the remaining five authorized strikes have been cast and are now in the possession of Baron Janssen in Belgium; Jardine, Matheson and Co., Ltd., the Connaught Centre, Hong Kong; the Künsthalle, Bielefeld, Germany; a private collection in France; and the sculptor, on loan to Leicester University in England.[5]

10   Masayuki Nagare
Japanese, born 1923

Stone Riddle
Dark granite   Executed in 1967; installed in 1972
Unsigned
Height: 64 inches; length: 37 inches (1 × 3 meters)
Location: courtyard of Engineering Quadrangle

In 1944, John B. Putnam, flight leader of a Thunderbolt fighter squadron over Western Europe, and Masayuki Nagare, a kamikaze pilot in the Japanese navy, were wartime enemies half a world apart. Putnam, killed in the conflict, was characterized by one who knew him well as "something of a woodland creature." Nagare, spared from a zero mission by the ending of the war, whiled away free time between combat duties observing the structure, texture, and beauty of a stone he had once picked up. How enigmatic that these men, ignorant of each other's being, should now be linked through a sculpture called *Stone Riddle* set among trees on the Princeton campus.

Nagare, like Putnam, was snatched from university studies to become a war ace. Born in Nagasaki in 1923, he spent his adolescence in Kyoto, first under the exacting rule of a Zen temple and later attending Ritsumeikan University, concentrating there on a classical education in Shinto, Buddhism, the traditional arts and crafts, and the ritual sports. Nagare chose a different pattern of life after the war. Roaming throughout Japan, he lived with fishermen, farmers, and laborers, seeking out stonecutters and artisans in remote villages to absorb a craftsman's knowledge of stone and sense of its essence.

Nagare then devoted his energies for some six years to working directly with stone, a regime that crystallized his conception of sculptural form. It must be kept in mind that the occupation of sculptor as known in the West did not exist in Japan until recent times. Reaching back to his experiences as a student and wanderer, and to his native antecedents, Nagare has forged a personal style in which there is no place for novelty or idiosyncrasy. His sculptures, as frequently left unsigned as signed, have a timeless character. "In ancient Japan," writes Nagatake Aso, "there were no divisions between the natural wonders of the earth and the objects made by man."[1] Nagare's twentieth-century "stones" respect this traditional canon.

Nagare held his first solo exhibition in Tokyo in 1955. While he sold nothing on this occasion, it and subsequent exhibitions in Tokyo and at the Staempfli Gallery in New York City[2] brought him to the attention of Japanese and American collectors and, more significantly perhaps, into the orbit of internationally recognized architects such as Philip Johnson and Minoru Yamasaki. As his first commissioned public work, Nagare executed the gardens and fountains for the Palace Hotel in Tokyo in 1961. In 1963, he received the coveted Japan Architectural Award, followed by the commission of one of his more dramatic worked stone environments, the near cyclopean walls for the Japanese pavilion at the New York World's Fair of 1964. Visually reminiscent of the tightly fitted, stone structures of pre-Columbian Peru, the walls of the compound covered an area of 1,400 square yards and were composed of 600 tons of stones sent from Japan. It was by far the most memorable complex designed for the fair.[3]

By 1966, under the increasing pressure of commissions at home and abroad, Nagare abandoned his practice of employing scattered locations throughout Japan as workshops, and settled on the island of Shikoku, where he built a house high on a promontory facing the Inland Sea of Japan. His studio was constructed nearby at Aji, the site of the stone quarries long prized in Japan for their hard granite deposits. The villagers and stonecutters of Aji are Nagare's neighbors, friends, and collaborators. Working with the local *Sekisho-jiku*, or stoneworker's

guild, and with the *Mingu-ren* (craftsmen-designers) of Takamatsu City, the artist has realized the kind of existence he sought during his earlier years of travel and study.

Nagare continues to exhibit and to execute major commissions both in America and Japan. In New York City, for example, his elegant *Bachi* adorns the Metropolitan Opera,[4] and a splendid stone piece commissioned for the World Trade Center can be seen at the east entrance plaza of the complex.

Like all other sculptures by Nagare, *Stone Riddle* is unique. Executed in 1967 in the black granite derived from the quarries of Aji, the design consists of two basic elements: a roughly fashioned, natural menhir, polished on one side of the rectangular shaft, which serves as the support for a precisely cut and polished, abstract form. An enigmatic sculpture, *Stone Riddle* initially appears as a hieratic image harboring undefined connotations. As Gordon Washburn has observed: "We never find, in any of Nagare's work, representational forms taken from the objective world . . . . The plainest hints of his sources of inspiration lie, perhaps, in certain of his titles—*Moon Tray, Wave Shadow, Wind Child*—all poetic refer-

ences to the world of nature."[5] But *Stone Riddle*, implying a question to which the answer is uncertain, may speak of man's uneasy relationship not only with nature, but with his own mind and spirit.

Stone Riddle is a sum of technical refinements that clearly indicates how fully Nagare "feels" the stone he employs. Edges, surfaces, and textures, joined with the formalism of the design as a whole, combine to create a work of art that is both sensuous and controlled in a remarkable balance of the *yin/yang* principle. Its location in the landscaped atrium of the Engineering Quadrangle enhances a work that asks for the viewer's quiet reflection and empathetic response. Placed on a circular dais built of earth and retained by a low wall of coursed, rough stones, Nagare's sculpture exists among clumped birch trees and thick ivy and appears indigenous in this natural setting.[6]

Though stone has been Nagare's primary material, he has worked equally successfully in bronze, stainless steel, wood, and occasionally in stonework tile. In addition to *Stone Riddle*, Princeton is fortunate to possess a bronze by Nagare, *Invocation*, dating from 1964.[7]

11 Louise Nevelson
American, born in Russia, 1900

Atmosphere and Environment X
Cor-Ten steel   Executed in 1969–1970; installed in 1971
Unsigned
Height: 21 feet; length: 16 feet (6.5 × 5 meters)
Location: between Nassau Street and Firestone Library

In describing her art, Louise Nevelson has written: "I do not belong to any movement. As my work is related to the present time, it is bound to be related to that of others, consciously or not, but I do not feel linked with any particular form of expression. I began to search for a reality that was not factual, a reality in an area where there was an unlimited source to reach what for me would be reality."[1] Nevelson herself and others have rightly acknowledged her various debts through the years, in greater or lesser degree, to the languages of Cubism, Constructivism, Dada, Surrealism, Assemblage, and Minimalism; her borrowings from Picasso, Miro, Arp, and Duchamp; her association with such peers as deKooning, Rothko, David Smith, Ad Reinhardt; her collecting of African art, American farm tools, architectural elements, and diverse other fragments of the past; and her attraction to the art, and especially the architecture, of pre-Columbian Mexico and Central America.[2]

From such an inventory of sources, it would appear that Nevelson was the "great eclectic" of twentieth-century sculpture. But such is not the case, for her style is remarkably individual and very much her own. She has matured slowly as a sculptor. Although she settled on wood as her special medium in the 1940s, Nevelson was well past the half-century mark when she began to create the extraordinary shadow-box reliefs and walls of wood that constitute her masterworks, and remain her most important contribution to twentieth-century art.

What then is it that makes Louise Nevelson such a singular artist and one so difficult to pin down stylistically? In Martin Friedman's perceptive words, her sculptures are:

> ...phantom architecture [which] allude to no single time or place ... even though fragments of orna-

mentation evocative of Doric and Ionic columns, baroque carving and Victorian finials, are embedded in their surfaces .... But if such enigmatic shapes inevitably suggest the antique and the dream world, it is the living city's forms that give meaning to her art .... Within it a spiritualized geometry prevails .... The sculptures are deepened picture planes and boxlike, shallow spaces filled with low relief arrangements. Because of their frontality, static quality, apparent weightlessness and Nevelson's obsession with surface, these tenuous shapes can best be considered within the context of illusionistic painting rather than in terms of conventional sculpture.[3]

The attributes that Friedman describes so convincingly—lack of historical reference, "spiritualized geometry," dissolution of volume, frontality, static orientation—suggest not so much the great traditions of Western art but rather the Orientalized art of Byzantium and its Russian derivatives. It is there, I believe, that lie the psychic origins of Nevelson's art. Consider also her penchant for rectilinear format in which shapes and patterns, rhythms and accents tend toward repetition and read in narrative fashion, together with her use of such "abstract" non-hues as black, white, and gold (equivalent to the space-erasing gold backgrounds of Byzantine mosaics and icons), and one finds the evidence too compelling to ignore.[4] In this context, it is not inconceivable to see a wall by Nevelson as a construction reminiscent of the *iconostasis*[5] of Greek or Russian Orthodox churches, or her shadow-box reliefs as suggestive of a *Pala d'Oro*.[6]

It must be said that Nevelson's own statements[7] suggest no conscious awareness of any stylistic ties with the art of Byzantium (or even with that of Russia), although the circumstantial evidence of an

Maquette, 1968, Cor-Ten steel, painted black,
14½″ (H). The Art Museum, Princeton University.
Gift of the artist

affinity seems to me sufficiently strong to warrant its statement here. One should note in this connection that Nevelson left her native Russia in 1904 at an age too young to be cognizant of the cultural and artistic traditions of her homeland. Other Russian emigré sculptors, such as Lipchitz, Gabo, and Pevsner, developed there in a climate where political and religious systems (and their attendant Russo-Byzantine style) had lost vitality and validity and were to be swept away shortly by revolution. These sculptors reacted against the past and rejected old national canons of style; Lipchitz embraced the tenets of Cubism while Gabo and Pevsner created their own Constructivist theories. Nevelson, meanwhile, was emerging as an artist in America where there was no equivalent national tradition to reject, and her mature style evolved long after the contributions of Cubism, Constructivism, and other pioneering

styles of early twentieth-century art had gained international acceptance.

Nevelson was in her seventieth year when in 1969 she undertook the Princeton commission for her first monumental outdoor sculpture in Cor-Ten steel. Although, in addition to wood, she had been working with plexiglass, aluminum, and different synthetics since the mid-1960s, Cor-Ten seemed at first a formidable material to employ for her work.[8] But she approached the problem with equanimity, and *Atmosphere and Environment X* became the first of a number of steel sculptures to be executed by her in the next decade.

Accustomed to developing her compositions by arranging and altering selected elements during the course of execution, Nevelson discovered that steel imposed new methods of working and some restriction on the freedom she had enjoyed with wood. A finished maquette that allowed no subsequent change was made before the technicians at Lippincott, Inc. could proceed with the fabrication of the monumental sculpture. The complexity of elements had to be simplified and the multiplicity of shapes and surface textures minimized. Compared with the range of motifs found in the wood constructions, the elements employed in *Atmosphere and Environment X* are fewer in number and curtailed in variety.

Constructed on a modular system, the work incorporates a judicious choice of shapes and enclosed forms—rectangular boxes and flat components of circular discs, half- and quarter-circles, rectangles, and undulating ribbon patterns. Basically a two-dimensional, architectonic screen, increased in depth by projections and setbacks, the sculpture achieves character and magic from the play of natural light over surface geometry. When the light is favorable to solid areas, the sculpture is boldly structural and earthbound; when voids are given their chance to emerge, it assumes a lacelike delicacy and weightlessness. Nevelson has termed herself variously an "architect of shadow," an "architect of light," and a "creator of reflections." She is all those things and, as we have seen, considerably more.

12   Isamu Noguchi
American, born 1904

White Sun
White marble   Executed in 1966; installed in 1970
Unsigned
Diameter: 28½ inches (.7 meters)
Location: lobby of Firestone Library

Born in Los Angeles in 1904, Isamu Noguchi is the son of a Japanese scholar-poet and an educator mother of Scotch-Irish and American Indian descent.[1] His many-sided artistic production has been equally cosmopolitan. Drawing on both Eastern and Western cultural traditions, Noguchi's sculptures appear to possess "effortlessness," a virtue Chinese artists once valued above perfection. But Noguchi's creative ease was acquired only through constant reinforcement of his inherent gifts by study and experimentation, which enabled him to assimilate into his own art many of the most subtle stylistic concepts of both West and East.

Taken to Japan at the age of two, Noguchi was educated there in international schools until he was sent back to attend high school in Indiana in 1918. Four years later, at eighteen, his artistic ambitions were temporarily sidetracked when Gutzon Borglum (who later carved the presidential portraits on Mount Rushmore, South Dakota) informed his young apprentice that he saw little hope of his ever succeeding as a sculptor. After two years of premedical training at Columbia University, Noguchi returned to sculpture, this time for good. He was elected to the National Sculpture Society at age twenty-one, and was awarded one of the first Guggenheim Fellowships in 1927. Deeply affected by the sculptures of Brancusi (then seen in a few choice galleries in New York), Noguchi departed for Paris and subsequently became Brancusi's assistant for two years. Brancusi's commitment to abstract art and his sensitivity to the materials of wood, metal, and stone fortified the younger man's natural predilections. Of the many influences that Noguchi absorbed and made his own in the evolution of his personal style, Brancusi's is perhaps the single most important one.

But other skills were needed to forge the *yin/yang* balance that Noguchi sought for his art. After a short return to the United States, the artist departed for the Far East to spend nearly a year renewing family ties and acquiring specialized knowledge that only Eastern traditions could provide. In Peking he spent several months under the aegis of the noted Ch'i Pai-shih (frequently called "the Matisse of China"), studying brush drawing and the structure of calligraphy in which he found strong plastic properties.[2] In Japan, he first sought to acquire his extraordinary knowledge of the ancient craft of ceramics, long revered and perfected in his paternal homeland.

Returning in 1932 to a New York City then suffering from the Great Depression, Noguchi helped to support himself by fulfilling portrait commissions. Among the most successful are expressive busts of George Gershwin, Buckminster Fuller, Martha Graham, and A. Conger Goodyear. It was in the 1930s that Noguchi also extended his range of talents into designs for modern furniture and lighting, stage sets for the dance of Martha Graham and for theater, and architectural plans for playgrounds and gardens. Few artists of the twentieth century have done more than Noguchi to achieve excellence in utilitarian design and quality for daily living by diffusing new aesthetic concepts.

Together with the numerous individual sculptures that have emerged from Noguchi's various studios throughout his long and distinguished career, the artist has been involved in major environmental projects, especially since the early 1950s. In 1951, he executed a garden for the *Readers Digest* complex in Tokyo and a memorial to his father at Keio University. In the following year, he designed a pair of

Isamu Noguchi
1904-
WHITE SUN, 1966
The John B. Putnam Jr. '45
Memorial Collection

Isamu Noguchi, *Sunken Courtyard*, 1960–64.
Beinecke Rare Book and Manuscript Library, Yale University

marble bridges symbolizing Life and Death for Hiroshima's Peace Park, laid out by Tange, Japan's celebrated postwar architect.

Since the *Jardins Japonais*, created between 1956 and 1958 for the UNESCO headquarters in Paris, Noguchi has executed many outstanding environmental designs in the West, collaborating with such leading architects as Buckminster Fuller, Louis Kahn, Marcel Breuer, and Gordon Bundshaft. Among the most notable of these achievements is the *Sunken Courtyard* of 1960–1964, fashioned in dazzling white Vermont marble, that accompanies Gordon Bundshaft's Beinecke Rare Book and Manuscript Library at Yale University. The Putnam Collection's *White Sun* is related to this work, as Noguchi explains:

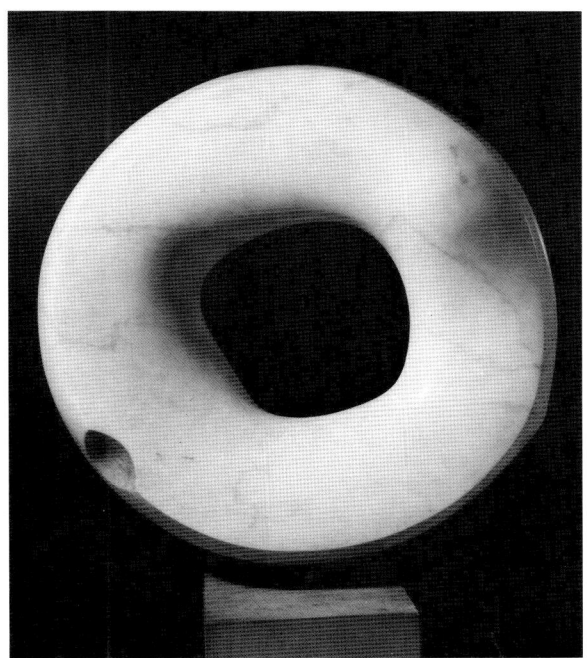

> At the time when I commenced work on the garden for the Beinecke Rare Books Library in 1961, I conceived of a sunken garden entirely of white marble. Within this composition were three elements—a pyramid representing the earth; a disque representing the sun; and a cube on its point representing chance. The process of development of this concept went through many phases, the cube having once been emergent from a pit with surfaces of various configurations. But it was the sun which gave me the most bother—to find something absolutely correct for the totality of the work. There must have been at least a dozen of them that I made—more or less complex. Then I made the various enlargements from my small models. The one that I finally selected for use at Yale exists in two different sizes: the 9′ 5″ at Yale, and two, I believe half-scale, one made in Vermont marble (similar to the final piece) and the other of cast iron taken from the original plaster.
>
> The *White Sun* at Princeton is one of the other studies that I made. This was carved by me in Italy at the same time that I made a somewhat different version of the study which is at the National Collection of Fine Arts in Washington [National Museum of American Art]. The latter is in a gray marble while yours is in statuary white. As I say, there were many studies made, among them was the one which is more modulated. This one is also made in two sizes. One I believe was half-scale and the other the full size of 9′ 5″, which is in front of the Seattle Art Museum and was carved in black Brazilian granite in Japan. It has been my conceit to think that I have spanned the continent with a giant *White Sun* in the East and a *Black Sun* on the western shores of America. May I say that Princeton's *White Sun* is among my favorites.[3]

White Sun was acquired for the Putnam Memorial Collection from the exhibition "New York Painting and Sculpture: 1940–1970" (no. 278), held at The Metropolitan Museum of Art in New York. It had been previously shown in the first retrospective exhibition of Noguchi's sculpture presented by the Whitney Museum of American Art in 1968 (no. 64).

13 Eduardo Paolozzi
British, born in Scotland, 1924

Marok-Marok-Miosa

Welded aluminum   Executed in 1965; installed in 1969
Unsigned
Height: 59 inches; length: 112 inches (1.5 × 2.9 meters)
Location: stairwell of Architecture Building

Early in his career, Eduardo Paolozzi established an ambivalent relationship with the far-reaching ramifications that the machine, modern technology, and mass media has had on popular culture in the second half of our century.

Born in Edinburgh, Scotland, in 1924 of Italian parentage, Paolozzi attended the Edinburgh College of Art before moving to London to study at the Slade School of Fine Art for three years. While enrolled there, Paolozzi spent as much of his time at the Science Museum drawing mechanical devices and engines as he did in the life class. Between 1947 and 1949, he experienced a productive and intellectually profitable two years living and working in Paris.[1] There he met Brancusi and Giacometti; and admired the readymades of Duchamp, the sculptures of Picasso incorporating found objects, and the magical drawings and collages of Max Ernst and Picabia. With Tristan Tzara as Nestor, he fed his strong interest in Dada and Surrealism on the rich resources of Paris. From Jean Dubuffet, he learned to appreciate the merits of *art brut*,[2] and later was to reveal in his own sculptures the influence of Dubuffet's fetishistic style.

Back in London by 1950, Paolozzi—who executed only a limited number of sculptures in the first half of the decade[3]—became an activist in the newly formed Independent Group affiliated with the Institute of Contemporary Art. Founded by avant-garde artists, art critics, musicians, architects, and photographers, the Independent Group sought to explore the ubiquitous effects of mass media on modern society.[4] A significant number of its ideas were subsequently to be realized in pop art and multi-media creations.[5] Similarly, the expressive range of collage and assemblage was considerably extended by artists in the Group, among whom Paolozzi played a key role.

In 1954 a screen-print entitled *Automobile Head*, in which individual motifs are all clearly distinguishable as automotive parts, heralded a new creative period for the artist.[6] The restricted scope of elements in the drawing was soon be be expanded by Paolozzi through what Sir Norman Reid has termed "the compendia of his fantasies and obsessions."[7] Sources for potential use in his work were collected and stored in scrapbooks filled with illustrations from technical and scientific journals, mail order catalogues, science fiction and movie magazines, pulp comic books, porno flicks, and advertisements.[8]

The persistent themes that have occupied Paolozzi in his sculptures, collage-graphics, and quizzical texts since the mid-1950s—man, objects, machines, and word images—are expressed in the cryptic captions he wrote for the scenario of his film *The History of Nothing* in 1962. "The history of painting, The History of the object. The history of man can be written with objects. All sculpture is a man-made object Machine as fetish Cylinder block Trojans column Laocoon As votive the crankshaft erotic Segments of information Enlarged mechanisms positioned carefully in a tiled interior"[9]

The bronze sculptures of the last half of the 1950s employed animal or human forms and bore such titles as *Monkey Man*, *Chinese Dog*, *Japanese War God*, or the names of such put-upon saints or heroes as St. Sebastian, Jason, and Icarus. But traditional connotations ended there. Reflecting a disdain for established canons of beauty and a scorn for tasteful aesthetics that Paolozzi shares with the Dadaists and Dubuffet, these new images of man were iconoclastic and brutally conceived. Creatures under duress,

they were robbed of humanity, clothed in the sludge of modern technology, and decorated with cast-off relics of the machine age. Nonetheless, these sculptures possess an awesome presence and an unforgettable clarity that places them among those "objects" essential for writing the "history of man" in our times.

In 1960, Paolozzi, then an artist of international reputation, was invited to become visiting professor at the Hochschule für bildende Künste in Hamburg.[10] Heavily industrialized through shipping enterprise, this teeming, aggressive center provided him for the next two years with an exhilarating experience equivalent to the one he had had in Paris more than a decade earlier. Already a savant of commercialism in modern manufacturing, Paolozzi discovered riches in the shipyards, steel plants, and salvage dumps of Hamburg, where he absorbed new visual images. Here he experimented with new techniques that were to reach fruition on his return to England.

While still in Germany, Paolozzi began to fabricate, for use in his own sculpture, plywood templates modeled after the normal industrial variety. He then had these templates cast in gunmetal, brass, and later in aluminum by professional industrial casters. The resulting flat plates and three-dimensional forms in the round were welded together to provide the structure of the sculpture and to serve additionally as decorative surfaces, key motifs, and projecting finials. This technique was employed almost exclusively for the series of architectonic *Towers* and *Idols* executed in the early sixties.

As a logical development, Paolozzi next undertook the assembly of sculptures from standard machine parts. He established his headquarters in a portion of the engineering works of C.W. Juby in Ipswich and took on a full-time welder as technical associate to assemble and weld stock components under his direction. When the desired shapes were not available from stock, Paolozzi's industrial casters in Fulham executed them as special orders from his drawings. Gradually, he found himself designing most of the components used in his sculptures.

Princeton's *Marok-Marok-Miosa* is one of three major works of 1965 in which most of the components were cast from the sculptor's designs.[11] Gone are the harsh, mechanistic character of the earlier *Towers* and *Idols*, and the disjointed and erratic sprawl of sculptures such as *Medea* (Rijksmuseum Kröller-Muller, Otterlo) of 1964. Instead, an almost baroque flow of overall surface and rhythms occurs, together with a greater control of spatial relationships; the sculpture is doubly realized as "object" and work of art. Seeking to remove association values from the observer's visual experience, Paolozzi has assigned a title to the assemblage that is provocative and ambiguous. Purposefully meaningless, it leaves the work free to speak for itself. Like all the sculptures of Paolozzi, *Marok-Marok-Miosa* is unique.

14 Antoine Pevsner
French, born in Russia, 1886–1962

Construction in the Third and Fourth Dimension
Bronze Executed in 1962; installed in 1972
Inscribed on one wing: *Pevsner 3/3*; on other wing: *Susse Fondeur. Paris*
Number 3 of edition of 4 cast in 1971
Height: 123 inches (3.12 meters)
Location: courtyard of Jadwin Hall

Construction in the Third and Fourth Dimension is one of the last major works of Antoine Pevsner, elder brother of Naum Gabo and collaborator with him in the creation of the Constructivist movement in Russia during the early 1920s.[1]

The sculpture was first executed in 1961 in an edition of three bronzes, 40½ inches high.[2] Pevsner had completed the plaster for the enlarged version and the designs for its pedestal before his death in 1962. From this plaster, four posthumous casts have been struck by the Susse Foundry in Paris under the authorization of Mme Pevsner;[3] Princeton owns no. 3/3 of these casts. The remaining casts are located at the Law School of the University of Chicago (no. 1/3); the Gemeenthe-museum, The Hague (no. 2/3); and the Jacques Lindon collection, Paris (no. 0/3). The right to an additional artist's proof was retained by the sculptor's widow. It is the intention of Mme Pevsner eventually to donate the original enlarged plaster to the Centre Georges Pompidou in Paris, to join the original bronze (first strike) of the smaller version of 1961, which she presented in 1962.

Older by four years than Naum Gabo,[4] Antoine Pevsner was born in Orel, Russia, in 1886. While studying painting at the academies of Kiev and St. Petersburg, Pevsner first became absorbed with concepts of space employed in the icons of churches and monastaries in Novgorod, and subsequently was attracted by the Impressionist and early School of Paris paintings in the remarkable Shchukin and Morozov collections in Moscow. Arriving in the French capital in 1911 in the heyday of Cubist invention, he was affected by its vigor but even more impressed by the engineering magic of the Eiffel Tower, with its superb relationships of skeletal solids and cavernous voids, all linked with elegance of style.

In Paris again in 1913–1914, he became friendly with Modigliani and Archipenko, and painted his first abstract picture in 1913.

Joining Gabo in Oslo during the early years of World War I, Pevsner continued as a painter but also became increasingly involved in the new sculptural theories and concepts of art being formulated by his brother. On their return to Russia in 1917, Pevsner was named, together with Kandinsky and Malévitch, a professor at the Academy of Fine Arts in Moscow. In 1920, Gabo and Pevsner were co-signers of their *Realistic Manifesto*, establishing guidelines for the Constructivist movement. But official support for innovative modes of artistic expression, which had at first existed in postrevolutionary Russia, soon proved to be short-lived. With the suppression of avant-garde art by the Soviets in the early 1920s, Pevsner joined his brother in exile. Settling eventually in Paris, he became a French citizen in 1930.

Though he had made his first "construction" in Berlin in 1923, Pevsner still regarded himself as a painter until he began seriously to experiment with Constructivist sculpture in Paris about 1925. By the early 1930s, he had achieved an independent and highly personal style. One major direction exploited the contortion of flat metal planes, theoretically capable of indefinite projection. Linear striations on the surface of the planes allow for the enjoyment of both spatial and temporal experiences simultaneously, while suggesting the possibility of infinite continuity. Pevsner called these shapes and surfaces "developable" and frequently employed the term in titles of his works.

The sculptor's mature style (epitomized in *Construction in the Third and Fourth Dimension*), has been described by Carola Giedion-Welcker as:

. . . the gradual relinquishing of clearly defined aerial spaces as well as of interpenetrating rectangular planes, in favor of great spatial curves which expand and contract, forming open vaults. The august dialogue with the limitless, with the unending, now opens with a fortissimo. The *Developable Surfaces*, indeed, develop to a point where these surfaces are expanded to the maximum, with the kinetics of the masses undergoing a much freer process of evolution than previously, abandoning all static conceptions. The dynamic, the monumental character of Pevsner's art, here find their special resonance, and the spatial phenomenon is transposed into a pure poetry of space.

The twisting of the planes is achieved here through a dense network of lines which transmit the movement to one another. The resulting curved planes with their fine structures seem to imprison space. These delicately structured webs of lines unfold before our eyes, revealing the genesis and the development of the curves in time.[5] These curved planes, whose chief function is to engage in a rhythmic game with space, to scan it by means of violent accents of light and shade, become animated by truly dramatic impulses . . . . Movement, here is not physically realized, as in Calder mobiles: it is the visual imagination which is solicited by the rhythm imposed on space.[6]

Among the honors and commissions accorded Pevsner internationally were a retrospective exhibition shared with his brother at The Museum of Modern Art in New York in 1948; a Second Award (again paralleled by Gabo) for his project in the international competition for the proposed monument to "The Unknown Political Prisoner" in 1953; monumental sculptures for the University of Caracas, Venezuela (1950), and for Eero Saarinen's General Motors Technical Center in Warren, Michigan (1955–1956); a retrospective exhibition at the Musée National d'Art Moderne in Paris, 1957, and a room of his sculptures at the twenty-ninth Venice Biennale in 1958; the award of the Legion of Honor in 1961. Two years after his death, the Musée d'Art Moderne

Antoine Pevsner, *Spatial Construction*, 1961 (first version), no. 1/3, 40½″ (H). Musée Nationale d'Art Moderne, Paris. Gift of Mme Pevsner

in Paris dedicated a gallery in honor of Pevsner in which a major portion of his life's work was assembled through a special gift from Mme Pevsner. In 1976 this superb representation of the artist's career was moved to the Centre National d'Art et de Culture Georges Pompidou, where it has been absorbed into the collections of the Beaubourg.

The Putnam Pevsner, with its handsome black granite pedestal designed by the sculptor, serves additionally as a memorial to the Danish scientist and humanist, Niels Bohr (1885–1962), who had longstanding personal and professional ties with colleagues in the Department of Physics at Princeton. Dedicatory inscriptions and a quotation from Bohr's 1950 letter to the United Nations,[7] enunciating the policy of an Open World, flank the paving stones at the base of the sculpture.

15 Pablo Picasso
Spanish, 1881–1973

Head of a Woman
Cast concrete   Executed by Carl Nesjar in 1971 from Picasso's maquette of 1962
Unsigned
Height: 16 feet; length: 12 feet (4.9 × 3 meters)
Location: entrance to McCormick Hall and The Art Museum

In his essay for the catalogue accompanying the exhibition "The Sculpture of Picasso," held at The Museum of Modern Art in New York in 1967, Sir Roland Penrose observed that Picasso possessed "a more personal attachment" to his sculpture than to his painting.[1] It is certain that he preferred to keep the major portion of his sculptures for his own collection, showed them infrequently to visitors, and rarely parted with unique pieces. It was only in his eighty-fifth year in 1966 that the artist agreed to include a comprehensive representation of his entire sculptural production in the major retrospective, "Hommage à Pablo Picasso," held at the Petit Palais in Paris. This was followed, in 1967, by the two successive exhibitions devoted solely to his sculptures and ceramics at the Tate Gallery in London and The Museum of Modern Art in New York. Included in all three exhibitions was the *Head of a Woman*, slightly larger than one foot high and created in Mougins in 1962,[2] which was eventually to serve as the inspiration for the monumental sculpture at Princeton.

This *Head of a Woman* is one of a considerable number of sculptures, mostly modest in physical scale, created by Picasso from the early 1950s until at least the mid-1960s. Constructed of cutout and folded sheet metal, and normally painted, nearly sixty of these maquettes were shown publicly for the first time in the Paris, London, and New York exhibitions of 1966–1967. Discerning in them one instance of the continuity characteristic of Picasso's work throughout his long lifetime, Penrose saw their genesis in the scissor and paper cutouts the young Picasso had made for the delectation of his sister, and in the torn-paper or wire follies he frequently created later for the diversion of his friends.[3] Eventually this persistent memory was dignified by Pi-

casso in the creation of these durable, and more serious, maquettes whose images he deemed capable of translation into monumental sculptures. Characteristic of these works is the exploitation of flat surfaces transformed by folding and bending into three-dimensional planes, which in turn envelop or penetrate surrounding space. Thus, through the genius of Picasso, the impromptu and imaginative inventions of childhood were transposed into works of art whose imagery and treatment of surface, planes, and space further enriched the vocabulary of twentieth-century sculpture.

One of the early goals of the Selections Committee was to initiate negotiations with Picasso that would lead to the acquisition of a major sculpture for the Putnam Memorial. Through committee member Alfred Barr, contact was made with Carl Nesjar, the Norwegian artist whose thirty-eight-foot-high realization in concrete of Picasso's *Bust of Sylvette* had recently been completed for New York University in lower Manhattan. Nesjar agreed to serve as intermediary with Picasso in the negotiations and to execute the sculpture if approval were granted.[4] Feeling that Picasso would be more receptive if he were presented with at least two possibilities for consideration, the committee selected *Head of a Woman* as first choice and *Sparrow Hawk*[5] as an alternate. Armed with site plans, *in situ* photographs of a composition-board mockup, and a letter of request from President Goheen, Nesjar visited Picasso at his home in the south of France in November 1969 and received his approval for the realization at Princeton of the monumental version of *Head of a Woman*. A photograph of the mockup, signed and inscribed "Bon à tirer pour Nesjar. Picasso. le 18.11.69," formed the contract beteen the artist and the University for the execution of the sculpture.[6]

Maquette, 1962, folded metal cutout, painted, 12⅝″ (H). Estate of the artist.

Before construction could begin, problems, both aesthetic and technical, had first to be resolved by Nesjar in collaboration with Picasso. Among the more important of these was an increase in the scale of the finished sculpture from that of the mockup. A decision also had to be made about the colors of the crushed stones to be employed in the realization of the sculpture by the *Naturbetong* technique developed in Norway in the mid-fifties.[7] Although a number of Picasso's sculptures had already been realized by this technique, Princeton's was the first to be developed from a multicolored maquette. In painting the diminutive original, Picasso had employed a consistent, rich cobalt blue for the large areas of the hair, and for the outline drawing of the eyes, brows, cheeks, nose, and mouth. A vibrant rose-red in crayon toned the cheeks and enlivened the sketchy hatch

marks on the face and columnar shaft. The remaining areas were left with the white prime coat.[8] Since nature is not richly endowed with non-gem blue stones, Nesjar selected with Picasso's concurrence a blue-black granite for the cobalt of the maquette and for the other color a quartzite ranging between rose and terra cotta; both stones were imported from the mountains of Norway.

The sculpture was created by Nesjar *in situ* on the green in front of The Art Museum over a five-month period in the summer and fall of 1971. The process involved initially the building of wooden forms to establish the basic shapes of the columnar pedestal (executed first and separately), and then a similar structure for the head itself. The forms of the latter possessed, on alternate sides, incised and appliquéd areas to create the relief drawing of facial de-

Contract with Picasso on photograph of mockup

tails and the strands of hair. After completion of the wooden form, a mixture of crushed stone—granite or quartzite depending on the desired areas of color— and iron tie-rods was packed within and then liquid concrete was injected under pressure from the base up. The rising grout filled all the interstices of the stone aggregate and was driven to the inside extremities of the form to create a flush, overall, smooth-textured surface when the wooden structures were removed. The column of the neck was built in place and the head, constructed independently, was hoisted onto it.

Once the concrete had cured sufficiently and the wooden form had been removed, Nesjar, armed with a powerful sandblasting jet, began exposing the textured aggregate within by blasting away the outer "skin" in appropriate areas to reveal the desired color and, additionally, to clarify and refine the details of drawing on the face and the cylindrical base. The back of the head was textured by the same blasting technique. Finally, all the concrete surfaces were cleaned with acid and given a coat of silicone to seal them.

Nesjar scheduled the completion of *Head of a Woman* to coincide with Picasso's ninetieth birthday. On this occasion, October 25, 1971, a celebration was held at the site to honor the master and his collaborator, and to signal the acquisition of a major work of art for the Putnam Memorial Collection and Princeton University.[9]

16 Arnaldo Pomodoro
Italian, born 1926

Sphere VI
Polished bronze   Executed in 1966; installed in 1969
Unsigned
Diameter: 48 inches (1.2 meters)
Location: courtyard of complex formed by Lourie-Love Hall and 1922, 1940, 1941, and 1942 Dormitories

Four years after Mussolini and his Blackshirts came to power in Italy, Arnaldo Pomodoro was born in 1926 at Morciano di Romagna near Pesaro on the Adriatic Sea. In the same year, the movement known as the Novecento (Twentieth Century) was founded in Milan. Though singularly devoid of vitality, it was to characterize semi-official Italian style until the collapse of Mussolini's regime in the mid-1940s. Ignoring the contributions made to international art by the Futurists and the Metaphysical school of De Chirico, the Novecentists emulated Fascist ideals of nationalism, conservatism, and traditionalism. Their influence cast a sterile pall over Italian art for more than two decades.

It is all the more phenomenal that the first generation of artists to arise in Italy after World War II should have rejoined the mainstream of modern art with such celerity and that so many should have achieved international status in the immediate postwar years: painters such as Afro, Birolli, Burri, Fontana, and Licini, and the sculptors Marino Marini, Manzù, Mirko, Consagra, Viani, and Greco. Though junior by a half-generation to most of these artists, Pomodoro and his younger brother Giò had the same cultural hurdles to surmount. Arnaldo attended technical school in Rimini and after the war acquired a basic knowledge of architecture and engineering in Pesaro. A strong predilection for drama, especially "Aeschylus, Brecht, and Sartre,"[1] led him into designing for the theater in Pesaro, sometimes with his friend Giorgio Perfetti as collaborator. Essentially a self-trained artist, Pomodoro began in the early 1950s, in conjunction with the tragically short-lived Perfetti, to create gold jewelry of exceptional quality. As the Gruppo 3-P, they exhibited first in Pesaro and subsequently at the Triennale in Milan and the Biennale in Venice, where they attracted an international clientele with their miniature treasures.

In 1954, the brothers moved to Milan, where they soon came to know other artists and critics, and where the city's leading avant-garde painter, Lucio Fontana, extended them generous support. Their first, modestly successful exhibitions of sculpture were joint efforts, held in Milan in 1954 and 1955, which brought them an invitation to participate in the Biennale in Venice in 1956. Thereafter, it was inevitable that the careers of Pomodoro and his brother, a sculptor of comparable distinction, should diverge.

While still living in Pesaro, Pomodoro had come across an illustrated monograph on the work of Paul Klee and had fallen under Klee's enchantment: "I started to draw like Paul Klee, really imitating his ideas and images. Incidentally, it was in this way that I discovered the technique of the negative forms which I later used in my castings of small plaques."[2] Recognizing the purposefully ambiguous nature of much of Klee's ideographic symbolism, Pomodoro invented his own syntax of abstract signs, which often superficially resembled undecipherable archaic glyphs. In his sculptured plaques, he endowed Klee's linear surfaces with plastic dimension, and honored his debt by entitling his reliefs *Homage to Klee*.[3]

Between the mid-1950s and mid-1960s, Pomodoro perfected his technique of casting in the negative/positive process, in which the artist works initially in clay or plaster, carving or gouging out his motifs as negative images; when cast these elements are reversed and transposed into the positive forms of the final sculpture. Pomodoro first developed the technique in his elegant cast jewelry, then extended it to his plaques and bas-reliefs in silver, lead, and

mixed media, and to monumental sculptures in bronze, steel, and other hard materials.

By the end of the 1950s, Pomodoro felt constricted by the limitations of the bas-relief.[4] His dissatisfaction grew during his travels in the United States in 1959–1960 and 1961, when he encountered David Smith and Louise Nevelson and formed ties with other artists and poets on the East and West coasts. But the transition in his work from flat relief to sculpture in the round was well under way before his American experiences.

It was in 1959 that Pomodoro made the first *Traveler's Column*, a glyph-filled relief in bronze with a curved surface. This anticipated his first fully realized sculpture in the round, the monumental *Traveler's Column* in iron, exhibited at the Spoleto Festival in 1962. Its upright cylindrical form persisted in Pomodoro's work, as has the title. His earliest experiments with cubes and spheres in sculpture date from 1961, and in 1963 Pomodoro executed what he describes as his "first successful sphere"—*Sphere No. 1* in the collection of The Museum of Modern Art in New York.[5]

The columns, spheres, and reliefs of this period were all characterized by an imagery of pure form sundered, violated, and partially eaten away by internal erosion. Now Pomodoro's signs and glyphs seemed to take on a life of their own. Beneath the flawless polished or natural skins of the exterior surfaces, multiple motifs of recessed and repeated dentils, ribs, and hatching became for the artist "an expression of an interior movement and thus of a movement of rupture or of splitting or of emptiness."[6]

During the academic year 1966–1967, Pomodoro was artist in residence at Stanford University. His months on the West Coast proved to be a fruitful experience for the sculptor, and it was there that he evolved the first of his new spheres, the *Rotanti* or *Rotors*, of which the Putnam Memorial Collection has one of the earliest examples. In these sculptures a central band divides fragmented hemispheres whose interior motifs now occur as formally ordered channels and projections, while still retaining evolutionary ties with their origins as autograph glyphs.[7] Earlier Pomodoro had described his spheres as "perfect, magic, closed form[s] into which I break to discover . . . the internal fermentation, mysterious and alive."[8] The distinction, he later explained, between the *Spheres* and the *Rotors* lay simply in the stability of the one and the potential mobility of the other.[9] The *Spheres*, that is, are intended to be seen on a fixed site; by contrast the *Rotors*, as their name suggests, are capable of being rolled from place to place, endowed with multiple, diverse, and equally valid views. Thus, Princeton's elegant *Sphere VI (Rotante Primo Sezionale)*,[10] though pinned to the earth for reasons of security, is vested with inherent mobility. While it functions superbly in its present role, the viewer should be aware of its latent potential for movement and for multiple changing images.

At the conclusion of an interview in 1974, Arnaldo Pomodoro expressed some deeply felt ideals: "I can enjoy my sculptures in a park, in an ancient public square, like Pesaro, or on a great university campus . . . . I like to see people lean their bicycles on the sculptures, and pigeons come to rest, to see them humanized . . . . For my work, I hope to strike a balance between an absolute artistic quality, as in a museum experience, and the sense of being in the midst of life, a part of its movement, and its hope for change."[11] *Sphere VI* at Princeton is a fulfillment of these words.

17 George Rickey
American, born 1907

Two Planes Vertical Horizontal II
Stainless steel   Number 3 of edition of 5
Unsigned
Executed in 1970; installed in 1972
Height: 14 feet 8¾ inches (4.5 meters)
Location: between East Pyne Building and Murray-Dodge Hall

Rickey's career has been that of a man who has played many parts. He was born in South Bend, Indiana, in 1907, his father a mechanical engineer and his grandfather a clockmaker. They endowed him with a precise and analytical mind, adeptness of hand, and an interest in mechanical virtuosity that was to become evident later in life. Taken to Scotland by his family in 1913, Rickey was educated there and at Balliol College, Oxford, where he took his degree in Modern History and where he also studied at the Ruskin School of Drawing. After traveling in Germany and studying painting in Paris with André Lhote, Léger, and Ozenfant, he returned to the United States to teach history for three years at Groton. The next three years were spent in Paris and New York, with a stint in the editorial department of *Newsweek Magazine*. In 1937 Rickey received the first Carnegie Award granted to an artist and became artist in residence at Olivet College in Olivet, Michigan, then a lively center for the arts.

The Second World War proved to be a real turning point for Rickey. Entering the Army Air Force in 1942, he became a computer specialist and, as he says, "discovered the mechanical side of me I'd overlooked." His first mobiles, constructed while in the army, made inevitable his gradual shift in interest from painting to sculpture. After the war, and until the 1960s, Rickey studied and taught art in various American universities, traveled in Mexico and Europe, and held exhibitions in New York City. During this period, he gradually consolidated his style through kinetic experiments with such materials as steel wire, glass, plastics, and ultimately steel.

According to Peter Selz: "While Calder's organic shapes suspended from wires approximate nature,

Rickey set out to investigate the behavior of movement itself."[1] In the *Realistic Manifesto* published by Gabo and Pevsner in 1920, Rickey recognized a logical springboard for investigations compatible with his theoretical and analytical turn of mind. Principle 5 of the manifesto had stated: "We affirm in these [plastic and pictorial] arts a new element, the kinetic rhythms, as the basic forms of our perception of real time."[2] Though Gabo himself executed few sculptures exploring actual movement, he continued to be a central apologist for the legitimacy and significance of kinetic art. In an interview in 1956, he said: "Constructive sculpture is not only three-dimensional, it is four-dimensional in so far as we are striving to bring the element of time into it. By time I mean movement, rhythm; the actual movement as well as the illusory one."[3]

Rickey has similarly incorporated the "element of time" through kinetic action into his sculptures. Although the elevation may not be noticed by the casual observer, *Two Planes Vertical Horizontal II* stands on the highest point of the Princeton campus. With planes balanced to spin in the breezes, each flashing, burnished blade can move in a complete 360-degree arc, depending on the velocity of the wind, while the entire upper assembly swings in counter movement, like a light-catching weathervane. Of the development of the sculpture, Rickey writes in a letter of April 30, 1975, to the author.

Having worked with moving lines for a decade or more, I began to consider the possibilities of moving surfaces. The lines dissected a planar space in a kind of kinetic drawing. Moving planes would occupy a volume rather than trace a silhouette.

violent winds because there need be no limit stops.... The geometry was kept as simple and obvious as possible; variety and complexity lay in the movement.

These first planes were made in a *Schlosserei* [sheet metal works] in Berlin, where I was a visiting artist during 1968–69 and again in 1970.... I taught my German colleagues how to spotweld the 1mm. stainless steel skin onto the frames. All the surfaces I finished myself with a sixty grit grinding disc in a random pattern which ... simply renders the surface more responsive to light. I myself adjusted the counterweights, the posture, and the period of the pendular swing. The first variation had squares 6′6″ by 6′6″ on the diagonal, then second version, vertical-horizontal. Then followed a smaller version, on a proportionately taller stem. This is the version at Princeton.

The planes are about 59″ × 59″ × 4″. Everything is stainless steel except the bearings and the counterweights (90 lbs. of lead in each unit). The planes are filled with styrofoam so that they will not echo or ring. The structure is welded except for the access doors to the bearings and counterweights which are screwed down.

Two Planes Vertical Horizontal II was made in an edition of five. I thought that, after investing a lot of time and effort in the initial production, I might follow the practice of bronze-casting sculptors with their editions of three, five, or eight, and have my *Schlosser* capitalize on his experience. One cannot have a new, worthwhile idea every day. Small editions make distribution easier and cheaper. Princeton's piece is the third of the five.[4]... A prototype, on which I learned, somewhat smaller, I have kept for myself.

My one-up-one-down knife-edge bearing system, very low in friction, was readily adaptable to these planes on a small scale and the larger "sail area" was responsive to the gentlest air currents indoors. Then I tried a larger scale, outdoors, in a sculpture for "Documenta IV" in Kassel, Germany in 1968, and substituted ball bearings for knife edges, thereby permitting the moving elements to turn through a full 360° around a horizontal axis. In addition, I mounted a pair of moving planes on a thrust bearing, permitting the whole assembly to turn through 360° around a vertical axis. This provided a new freedom, a visually more complex choreography, exposure to the endless supply and variety of the outdoor breeze, and security from

In the development and enrichment of kinetic art, Rickey has been the most inventive Constructivist explorer of his generation. With his book *Constructivism: Origins and Evolution* (1967), he has also written the most definitive and acute analysis of the movement and its ramifications to date.

18 George Segal
American, born 1924

Abraham and Isaac: In Memory of May 4, 1970, Kent State University
Bronze   Executed in 1979; installed in 1979
Unsigned
Height: 81 inches; length: 112 inches
Location: between Chapel and Firestone Library

George Segal's *Abraham and Isaac: In Memory of May 4, 1970, Kent State University* is atypical of the work he has produced in the twenty-year span during which he has become an internationally renowned sculptor. Although Segal's public outdoor bronzes have been made only in the last few years[1] and are not as well known as his plaster figures, it is the subject of the Princeton bronze sculpture, more than its medium and site, that distinguishes it from most of his work. The sculpture depicts a specific Biblical story and commemorates an actual event in recent American history, the National Guard shooting of students demonstrating against the Vietnam War at Kent State University.

The typical Segal sculpture avoids such specificity in terms of subject matter. It is usually a life-size plaster figure (or figures), situated with or within actual objects of the real world, such as old furniture, windows, doors, or familiar utensils. The figures perform common, everyday acts. Although the figures are cast from living models, they remain anonymous and mute.

Segal's figures show arrested motion and weighty repose. They seem caught in a moment of stasis, and balanced between an act or sentence just completed and the unquestioned prospect of more of the same. We never encounter crisis, a critical moment, an apotheosis, or a decisive act. The narrative, if any, is held to a minimum. Instead, we are shown bodily routine, a state of mind, a random moment in time. There tends to be a minimum of specific and a maximum of general information. This explains why Segal's figures strike us as low-key, and always appear silent.[2]

They are private, involved within themselves, which compels us to accept them as the sculptor's personal statements made public.[3] The Princeton sculpture as we shall see is Segal's public statement made personal.

For most of his bronzes, Segal has placed his private sculpture in public places, relying on larger actual props and settings to turn these works into public monuments. An exception is the Princeton bronze, which contains no physical objects from the non-art world. The original plaster sculpture, from which the bronze was cast, has only a knife and a rope, but even these items now have been converted to metal. Even the rocky ground on which the figures of Abraham and Isaac stand is bronze. Segal has substituted a cultural prop, the story of Abraham and Isaac, in the place of actual objects, which explains their relative absence. As a consequence, he relates this work to the ancient heroic tradition in sculpture, which his work otherwise opposes. Instead of the figures performing a familiar activity, *Abraham and Isaac* depicts a familiar story, linking it to a sculptural heritage that enables it to become a genuine public monument transcending the artist's private expression.

The Princeton bronze is Segal's second version of the story, first treated in a 1973 plaster sculpture in Tel Aviv "in honor of the new nation" of Israel.[4] Like the Princeton sculpture, originally offered to Kent State University, which deemed it too provocative a memorial to accept, this sculpture also met with resistance because the image was seen at first as inappropriate to the theme.[5] However, Segal was attempting to suggest the miracle of the birth of Israel and the faith of its people. In the Princeton sculpture, Segal, using the same imagery, shifted his emphasis to commemorate not a joyous but a tragic event.

The only other Biblical story Segal has illustrated

George Segal, *The Execution*, 1967, plaster and wood, 8′ × 12′ × 8′. Courtesy, Sidney Janis Gallery, New York

within his mature period is the story of Lot, in a 1966 plaster sculpture entitled *Legend of Lot* (Walker Art Center, Minneapolis). Segal also dealt with this theme in a number of early sculptures, as well as paintings and drawings. These works reveal Segal's fascination with the theme of an individual faced with performing an act opposed to accepted morality for a supposedly higher purpose. In the 1966 sculpture, one of Lot's daughters seduces her drunken parent "that we may preserve seed of our father"[6] while the other daughter looks on silently. Similarly,

in the Princeton sculpture, Abraham, commanded by God to murder his only son to prove his faith, stands transfixed in his own terrible dilemma and looks on unspeaking. In a recent interview, Segal said of Kent State: "... it was a violation of habitual values. I was commissioned to commemorate that fact. I started to think about it and the leap I made in my own mind was to associate the Old Testament, Abraham-Isaac story with that event."[7]

The 1973 sculpture, a more straightforward rendering of the story, presents a patriarchal Abraham, large and bearded, his corpulent torso uncovered. A youthful Isaac, soft and feminine, hands bound behind him, lies meekly on his back on the same craggy ground that supports both sculptures. With the knife hidden by his thigh, Abraham seems to hesitate, for according to Segal, he "schemes . . . to substitute a ram as the sacrificial offering."[8] Borrowing this version of the story from Sören Kierkegaard, Segal emphasizes the miraculous and the need for faith.

Segal has indicated that he read Kierkegaard's *Fear and Trembling* in 1973 while making the first version of the sculpture: "Read *Fear and Trembling*. Head full of Kierkegaard's feverish replay of all the possible thoughts in Abraham's head on the trip to murder his son. Which was right? No matter."[9]

Kierkegaard's book also influenced the second version of the sculpture, but in this work Segal is not so much concerned with Kierkegaard's study of faith through the example of Abraham but with his brilliant variations depicting Abraham's inner conflict. In the Princeton version, Segal has Isaac kneel, hands tied in front, a more conscious young man. He has greatly diminished the bulk of Abraham, moving his leaner figure closer to Isaac. He has given Abraham a shirt and has him bluntly expose the knife. The Princeton figures form a more resolved, dignified composition in keeping with the psychological extremity of the scene and the aspect of the Kent State commemoration. However, despite the public function of this sculpture, Segal, by focusing intently upon Abraham's dilemma, has maintained the introspective quality so characteristic of his work in general.

Some of Segal's plaster figures have been compared to mythical creatures, for instance the famous *Bus Driver* (The Museum of Modern Art) to Charon, the ferryman of the dead.[10] Yet any such comparisons are the personal associations of the viewers since the sculptures seldom contain direct mythical references. It is their unreal appearance in everyday circumstances—a large plaster bus driver sitting in a real bus driver's seat with a steering wheel—that gives these sculptures their great evocative power. The reverse happens with the two figures that Segal identifies as Abraham and Isaac. Not only do we know they were cast from living people, but because they look like our contemporaries and not like mythical or heroic figures, they make us participants in the sculpture's disturbing drama.

In contrast to Segal's earlier work, we *do* witness a distinct critical moment in the Princeton sculpture when Abraham confronts the bound Isaac with the drawn knife. This disconcerting and initially misleading image, though it exposes the horror of violence, has no literal relationship to the Kent State shootings, nor does it exploit the violence of Kent State (we must remember, as Segal reminds us, that Abraham does not kill Isaac).[11] The conflict represented is not betwen father and son, but actually within Abraham.

We noted earlier that Abraham looks on in silence. As Kierkegaard states, Abraham's task is so inexplicable, he must remain silent. This silence, characteristic of Segal's introspective figures, is no doubt part of the sculptor's attraction to Abraham. In fact, Segal is so preoccupied with Abraham's turmoil, that he has chosen artists to pose for the two Abrahams, an Israeli artist for the earlier version and his friend Lucas Samaras for the Princeton piece, suggesting his own identification with Abraham.

In 1967, Segal created a more violent sculpture, *The Execution* (Vancouver Art Gallery), graphically displaying four victims of some unknown political or war-related shooting. *The Execution* is certainly mindful of episodes like Kent State, but Segal surpasses its stridency with a profound pathos in the Princeton *Abraham and Isaac*. Locked in an unresolved confrontation, the figures never relinquish their intensity and impact, which often does happen to images that shock. Segal has elevated the suffering of Abraham and the innocent Isaac into symbols of human anguish over the violence we commit upon others, the violence that is within ourselves.

Robert Lafond

19 David Smith
American, 1906–1965

Cubi XIII
Stainless steel   Executed in 1963; installed in 1969
Inscribed on base: *Cubi XIII   David Smith   Mar-25 1963*
Height: 114 inches (2.8 meters)
Location: lawn of Spelman Halls

Although David Smith resented a modern architecture that denies serious roles to sculpture and painting in contemporary building,[1] his competitive instinct would have been excited by the location of his *Cubi XIII* at Princeton. Placed in a natural surrounding of the trees he loved, it looks back on a group of dormitories that, like Smith's sculpture, owes a considerable debt to Cubist precepts. Designed by I. M. Pei and Partners and constructed in 1973, the Spelman Halls complex is composed of eight interlocking geometric buildings that vary in size and shape but remain constant in human proportion. The juxtaposition of two such original creations in architecture and sculpture, each demonstrating the continuing vitality of Cubist tradition more than a half-century after its inception, provides an exceptional experience for the eye and mind.

David Smith began seriously to exploit the potentialities of stainless steel as a medium in the late 1950s. From 1961 until his tragic death in 1965, he employed this material for the creation of his *Cubi*, a brilliant series of some twenty-eight sculptures that were destined to become the capstone of his career. Admired at the time for their invention and originality, they acted as a potent influence on another generation of artists preoccupied with Minimalist aims and theory.

Constructed of elementary geometric motifs, principally of cubes, rectangles, and cylinders used as volumetric or planar forms, the *Cubi* project an illusion of monumental size while retaining near-human scale. Many are complex in the number and arrangement of their elements. Others, like Princeton's *Cubi XIII*, are distinguished for the economy of means that produces a singular image of strength.

The anthropomorphic content that permeates many of Smith's works was noted by Edward Fry at the time of the artist's retrospective exhibition in 1969,[2] a feature shared by *Cubi XIII*. Smith was an intensely human figure—brusque in convictions, but tender in his relationships with others and in his sensitivity to the natural world. It was entirely in character for him to infuse the cool objectivity of Cubism and Constructivism with anthropomorphic reference. Fry sees the Princeton sculpture as a "semaphore signal-figure,"[3] but its nature is considerably more subtle. Seen in the kind of outdoor setting the sculptor envisaged for it, *Cubi XIII* assumes a physical warmth and a living presence that could well turn cold and metallic in an impersonal interior space. Like the human personality, it too has attributes that are variable and textural. It was David Smith himself who said:

> I like outdoor sculpture, and the most practical thing for outdoor sculpture is stainless steel, and I make them and I polish them in such a way that on a dull day, they take on the dull blue, or the color of the sky in the late afternoon sun, the glow, golden like the rays, the colors of nature. And in a particular sense, I have used atmosphere in a reflective way on the surfaces. They are colored by the sky and the surroundings . . . . They are designed for outdoors.[4]

Like all the sculptures in the series, *Cubi XIII* is fully named, signed, and precisely dated on the day of completion in forthright script applied with a soldering iron on the base of the work. Essentially a sculpture *en deux faces*,[5] the brilliancy of its polished steel surface evokes the sensuous delight offered

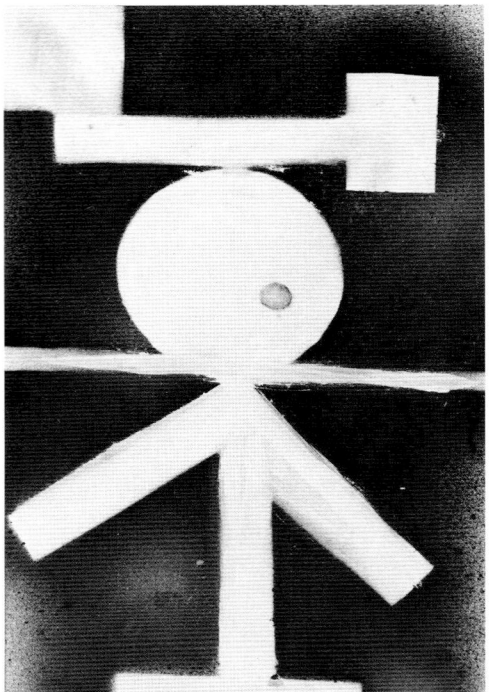

David Smith, study for *Cubi XIII*, 1963, painted and sprayed stencil drawing, 18″ × 12″. Estate of the artist (Courtesy, Knoedler Contemporary Art, New York)

by a freshly minted silver coin that courts investigation of its reverse image. The burnishing is lively and free, and the light-catching tracks left by the tool parallel the fluid brushwork of Abstract Expressionist painters. Equally pictorial is the use of a compositional device often favored by the sculptor: a narrow horizontal bar placed near mid-height creates a new elevated groundline and thus the illusion of a canvas on an easel. Within this implied pictorial area, an open space framed by the horizontal bars at top and bottom, Smith has placed his sparkling flat, stainless steel disk to serve as a central motif. Degrees of depth, both real and fancied, within the putative picture plane are established by the play of the capping rectangular bar and its satellite, counterbalanced cubes. This abstract, pictorial fantasy is visually directed back to the true groundline of earth by oblique tangent bars that radiate downward from the central disk.

David Smith began his career as a painter and continued to paint and draw throughout his lifetime.[6] As he said himself: "I do not recognize the limits where painting ends and sculpture begins."[7] Many of his finest metal sculptures were in fact created with the intention of being painted, and he executed this job with inordinate care and deliberation. When he spoke of the way in which his polished *Cubi* reacted to the hues of nature, it was with a true painter's sensibility. This dual aspect of his work has been well expressed by Jane Harrison Cone: "The strangeness of Smith's sculpture—perhaps singularity is a better word—its beauty and also its limitations have to be seen within this context of an artist who was manifestly and superbly a sculptor yet whose impulse was that of a painter."[8] Coming to sculpture as a painter, David Smith had little

propensity for modeling or carving and used a welding torch to execute his sculptures directly in iron or steel. His large corpus of works was achieved practically single-handed. Like all his sculptures, *Cubi XIII* is unique.

Since Smith's working method involved direct attack on his materials, much of his extraordinary invention occurred during the course of execution. As a substitute for preparatory maquettes, he relied for a long time on quick sketches made constantly from nature, or on rough and vigorous working drawings prepared for specific projects. By the late 1950s, however, when he was embarking on the *Cubi* series, he had evolved a speedy method of producing what might be called pictorial maquettes— "arrangements and assemblages of forms—rectangles of cardboard, crescents of watermelon rind, metal rods—that are momentarily 'fixed' on the page with a spray of paint, . . ."[9] A small number of these painted, mixed-media stencils, perhaps two or three, were made for some of the individual pieces in the *Cubi* group. According to the executors of the Smith estate, the stencil for *Cubi XIII* is unique.

Prior to its acquisition for the Putnam Memorial in 1969, *Cubi XIII* was shown at the Tate Gallery in London in the exhibition "'54–'64: Paintings and Sculptures of a Decade" in the spring of 1964, and, during 1966–1967, in the exhibition "David Smith: 1906–1965," organized by The Museum of Modern Art in New York and later circulated in Europe.[10] After its purchase and before it was installed on the Princeton campus, the sculpture figured in the retrospective exhibition of 1969, which from The Solomon R. Guggenheim Museum in New York City went to the Dallas Museum of Fine Arts and the Corcoran Gallery of Art in Washington, D.C.

20 Tony Smith
American, 1912–1980

Moses

Painted mild steel   Model executed 1967–1968; fabricated and installed in 1969
Unsigned
Number 1 of edition of 2
Height: 15 feet; length: 11 feet 6 inches (4.6 × 3.5 meters)
Location: grounds in front of Prospect

Born in South Orange, New Jersey in 1912, Tony Smith had roots that lay deep in the Newark area. His heritage there included a nineteenth-century ancestor who carved altarpieces for the city's churches, and later forebears who developed both materials and mechanical inventions that aided in the early development of the skyscraper as well as other innovative constructions of the early twentieth century. Since 1962, all his major sculptures were fabricated by his longtime collaborator, the Industrial Welding Company of Newark.

Smith worked first as a toolmaker and draftsman while studying painting and drawing at the Art Students League in New York City and later at the Chicago Bauhaus. But his innate interest in objects soon led him to architecture. After serving as clerk for Frank Lloyd Wright on a number of houses and spending some months at Taliesen East in Wisconsin, he managed his own successful independent practice for almost two decades. By 1960, however, he turned definitively to sculpture because of the need to find a more personal medium for expressing his preoccupation with the geometric relationships existing between form and space.

A strong and individual stylistic identity was early established. Though he was quickly recognized by such artist-peers as Pollock, Still, Rothko, and Newman, broader critical and public recognition came more slowly. At the time of Smith's first one-man exhibition at the Wadsworth Atheneum in Hartford in 1966, curator Sam Wagstaff could quite properly cite him as "one of the best known unknowns in American art."[1] More recent exhibitions and publications, plus a number of commissions for large-scale works such as *Moses* in the Putnam Memorial Collection, have secured his place as a significant contributor to the history of twentieth-century art.

Tony Smith worked deliberately and unhurriedly. After conceptual drawings, a maquette, variable in size but normally completely realized, was constructed in plywood or an equivalent substance. From this model, a larger or full-scale mockup of equally provisional material was frequently constructed, depending on whether the artist needed a lightweight piece for exhibition purposes or a model for preliminary study prior to its execution in steel. Once a sculpture was commissioned, the initial model was sent to the Industrial Welding Company for full-scale enlargement and fabrication. In exhibitions of the mid-1970s, smaller scale, finished works in steel, possessing their own conceptual identities, have appeared in Smith's oeuvre, but these, like the maquettes, are easily conceivable on an expanded scale.

Unlike many of his contemporaries who favor the heavier and tougher Cor-Ten steel for their sculptures, Tony Smith prefered mild steel. Lighter in weight for the same thickness, mild steel comes from the factory with a less wavy texture, making it easier to manipulate and to maintain exactly level planes. Moreover, mild steel accommodates itself more readily to welding than Cor-Ten steel, with the result that greater unity is possible in the joining of planes, a requirement essential to the character of a Tony Smith sculpture.

In replying to an inquiry about the relevance of subject matter in his work and the significance of the title *Moses*, Tony Smith wrote:

My sculptures are always conceived and developed as abstract geometric structures. None was created with subject matter in mind, nor has had

Maquette, 1967, pressed board, painted black, 22¾″ (H).
The Art Museum, Princeton University.
Gift of the artist

Construction at the Industrial Welding Company of Newark

Rembrandt, *Moses Smashing the Tablets of the Law.*
Staatliche Museen Preussischer Kulturbesitz,
Gemäldegalerie, Berlin

a title assigned to it before or while it was being
done. They were given titles only after a maquette
(at least) had been made. In some cases the work
had already been put together as a full-scale
mockup (e.g., *Willy*) or fabricated in steel (e.g.,
Free Ride) before its image became clear and it
was named. Occasionally titles were taken from
remarks made in discussing a piece, and more
often they came to me all at once. *Moses* is an
instance of the latter.

Associations with representations of the biblical Moses manifested themselves simultaneously
in the finished work to me, and resulted in its
title. The parallel uprights suggested the horns in
Michelangelo's *Moses*. We know that these strange
attributes were the result of a misunderstanding
by the Latin Vulgate of the Hebrew word "shone,"
derived from the word meaning "horn," and used

figuratively to denote rays or flashes of light proceeding from a luminous object, e.g., the head of Moses. The Vulgate, accordingly, through mistranslation, says of Moses' face that it was *cornuta*. This resulted in Michelangelo's peculiar representation of a horned Moses. My sculpture, without previous intent, perpetuates this curiosity but only after the fact of the finished work.

The same elements, the parallel uprights, evoked the raised arms of Moses as he shows the Tables of the Law, or is about to break them, as seen in Rembrandt's painting in Berlin. The first reproduction I saw of this picture was a detail showing the skyward reach of the arms but only as much of the slabs as was held by the hands. Most of the torso was as it appears in the rest of the painting. The large frontal plane in the sculpture, generally and its blackness, was associated with the folded tablets, and by position and somewhat in size and shape with the front of Moses' tunic. Hence the

identity of the inverted mirror image of the tablets with the tunic.

Besides the literal but chance combination of the elements in the sculpture itself, because of being composed of a free arrangement of already formalized components, this portmanteau telescoping of features has, for me, something of the two-dimensional configuration of the Chinese written character. This graphic reading, however, contrasts with the changing values in color under varying light conditions which are more consonant with the exalted examples of Western art cited, and with the plastic qualities of sculpture.[2]

As a coda, Tony Smith left the observer of his sculptures with a prescription for heightened visual experience: "If you think of space as a solid, my sculptures are voids in that space."[3]

A second version of *Moses* was acquired in 1975 for the city of Seattle, Washington.

21 Kenneth Snelson
American, born 1927

Northwood II
Stainless steel   Executed in 1970; installed in 1973
Unsigned
Height: 100 inches (2.5 meters)
Location: Proctor court, Graduate College

Kenneth Snelson's special concepts of space and structure are expertly realized in Princeton's *Northwood II*, a unique sculpture dating from 1970.[1] The original concept occurs in a macro-sculpture entitled *Lorraine* first shown in the Annual Sculpture Exhibition held at the Whitney Museum of American Art in 1968 (no. 115), and later acquired for the Hirshhorn collection. Snelson next created a larger structure for Northwood Institute in Texas, which he named *Northwood I* in deference to the institute. Since the artist attaches little importance to titles, he gave the same name to Princeton's sculpture, and once more to *Northwood III*, a structure shown in 1975 in a one-man exhibition of the artist's work held at Waterside Plaza in New York City and subsequently at the Stedelijk Rijksmuseum in Amsterdam, which also acquired a second version of the sculpture for its collection. A number of small maquettes exist for both *Northwood II* and for *Northwood III*.

Northwood II is deceptively simple. Six stainless steel tubes, of equal length and arranged in three pairs of oblique staggered parallels, appear to float in a geometric network of steel cables. These bind the tubular elements into a system which not only defines an internal space within the sculpture, but also relates that space with the surrounding atmosphere.

Snelson has defined his work as "a dialogue between push and pull" or a "conflict between tension and compression."[2] In the Putnam sculpture, as in all his major structures, the tubes exert compression "push" (seemingly causing them to float) while the steel cables set in motion tension "pull." So cohesive is the integrity of the structure that removal of one member would cause the whole to collapse in a meaningless mass. In a letter to the author, Snelson has elaborated on his work:

When I direct my attention toward sculpture, I concern myself with the actual physical forces which give rise to the form. The necessary ingredients of my kind of space are the minimum number of lines of force which must be present in order for the system to exist. In previous methods or approaches to space, this was not considered at all. Structure was something to be thought of after the visual matters had been satisfactorily stated. What I present, finally, is a force diagram made visible. . . . The forces become visible as they occupy and are occupied by material elements. This is not unlike the use of iron filings which reveal a magnetic field. Instead of magnetic forces, we are speaking of tension and compression forces, or pull and push, as we know them from other experiences.[3]

In the assembly of a Snelson sculpture the elements are first laid out in the area of construction. The cable segments are previously cut to predetermined lengths. Each segment connects the ends of two of the tubular compression members. As additional cables are added and secured within the tubular ends and as the slack is taken up with a hand-winch, the structure begins to rise, take shape, and assume the character of the finished work. Each element effects a structural as well as an aesthetic order in the total assembly.[4]

Until his first one-man show in New York in 1966, Kenneth Snelson's "structures"—as he prefers to call his sculptures—were too often viewed as constructions related to science, engineering, or technology rather than to the aesthetic experience.[5] Since his milestone exhibition of tensile metal structures in Bryant Park, New York City, in 1968, however, the artist's sculpture has received wide recognition

![Easy Landing sculpture at Baltimore Inner Harbor]

Kenneth Snelson, *Easy Landing*, 1977, stainless steel, 35′ × 65′ × 85′.
Commissioned by the City of Baltimore for Inner Harbor

Maquette, 1969, aluminum and steel wire, 13³/₁₆″ (H)

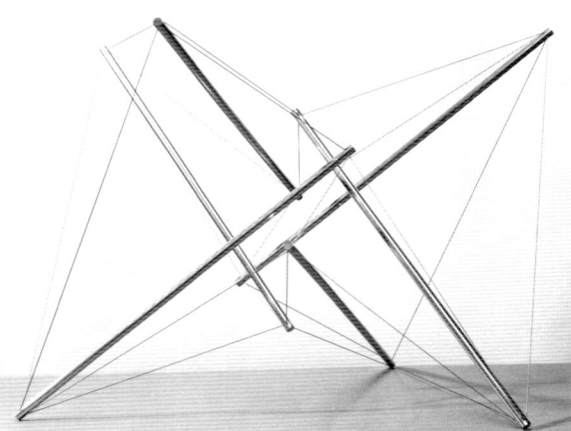

both in the United States and in Europe, and is represented in numerous collections.[6]

In 1977 a major assembly of the artist's structures was exhibited at the National-Galerie in Berlin and at the Wilhelm Lehmbruck Museum in Duisberg, Germany. In the same year Snelson's largest and most dramatic outdoor sculpture, entitled *Easy Landing*, was commissioned by Baltimore for installation in the city's inner harbor. Like the early constructions of Naum Gabo over a half a century earlier, Snelson's achievements propel the vision of twentieth-century man into a new perception of form and space, in terms not only of sculpture, but of the cosmos as well.

Locations of the Sculptures

The John B. Putnam, Jr., Memorial Collection

1 Reg Butler, *The Bride* (E2)

2 Alexander Calder, *Five Disks: One Empty* (H5)

3 Jacob Epstein, *Professor Albert Einstein* (H5)

4 Naum Gabo, *Spheric Theme* (K2)

5 Michael David Hall, *Mastodon VI* (F6)

6 Gaston Lachaise, *Floating Figure* (A6)

7 Jacques Lipchitz, *Song of the Vowels* (G2)

8 Clement Meadmore, *Upstart 2* (J2)

9 Henry Moore, *Oval with Points* (F2)

10 Masayuki Nagare, *Stone Riddle* (K2)

11 Louise Nevelson, *Atmosphere and Environment X* (G2)

12 Isamu Noguchi, *White Sun* (G2)

13 Eduardo Paolozzi, *Marok-Marok-Miosa* (G3)

14 Antoine Pevsner, *Construction in the Third and Fourth Dimension* (H5)

15 Pablo Picasso, *Head of a Woman* (F3)

16 Arnaldo Pomodoro, *Sphere VI* (F5)

17 George Rickey, *Two Planes Vertical Horizontal II* (F3)

18 George Segal, *Abraham and Isaac: In Memory of May 4, 1970, Kent State University* (G2)

19 David Smith, *Cubi XIII* (E5)

20 Tony Smith, *Moses* (G3)

21 Kenneth Snelson, *Northwood II* (B6)

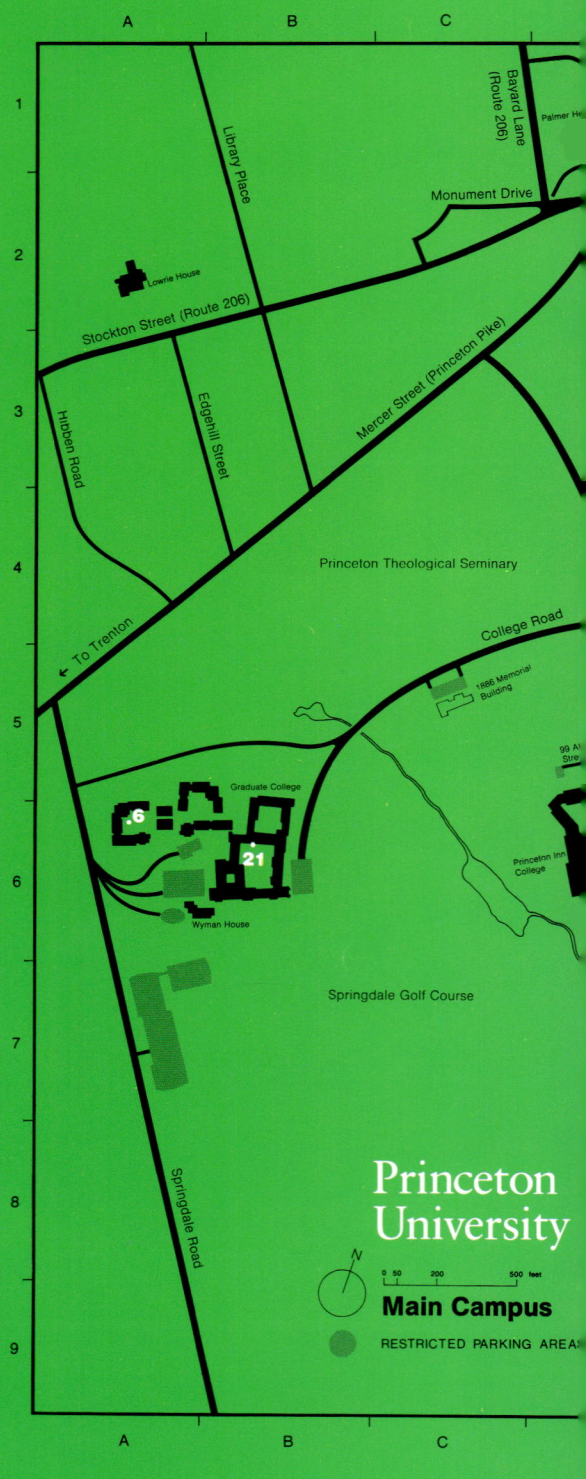

E F G H J K L M

Chambers Street

Palmer
Square

Witherspoon Street

Spring Street

South Tulane
Street

Vandeventer
Avenue

Moore Street

Nassau Street

Chestnut Street
(Highway 27)

Pine Street

Maple Street

Linden Lane

To New Brunswick →

1

Holder

Maclean House

Henry House

.11

Burr

Firestone Library

Olden Street

Engineering
Quadrangle

Murray Place

Aiken Avenue

Princeton Avenue

2

on
Joline

Stanhope

Student Center

.12

Campbell

Alexander

Nassau Hall

Green

185 Nassau Street

William Street

8

.9

West College

.7

.18

Biochemical
Sciences

Princeton University
Press

10 **4**

Von Neumann

Patton Avenue

Blair

17 East Pyne

Chapel

Dickinson

Frick Lab

Corwin

Manuscript
Library

Third World
Center

3

University
Store

Lockhart

Witherspoon

Clio

Whig

Murray-Dodge

McCosh

.15

Architecture

.13

1879

Woodrow Wilson School

Dial Colonial Tiger Elm

Prospect Avenue

Foulke

Edwards

McCormick

Dod

Art Museum

.20

Woolworth
Center

Prospect

Campus Tower

Quadrangle Ivy Cottage

Cap &
Gown

Cloister Charter

Stevenson Halls

Broadmead Street

Henry

Brown

Prospect
Gardens

Palmer

21 Prospect Ave

Roper Lane

4

1901

Cuyler

Jones

Terrace

70 Wash. Rd.

Computer Center

Pyne

1903

Walker

1937

McCosh Infirmary

Guyot

5 Ivy Lane

Ivy Lane

Western Way

Spelman Halls

Dillon
Gymnasium

Gauss

1939

Eno

Vivarium

Peyton

Strubing Field

171 Broadmead

19.

Tennis

Wilcox

1938

Greenhouse

Fine

.3

Clarke Field

FitzRandolph Road

5

New South

Tennis Pavilion

Courts

Lourie-Love

.16

1941

1922

Rock Magellanic Lab

.2

.14

Jadwin

Palmer Stadium

Finney Field

Campbell Field

Fields

Sexton

Baker Rink

1940

1942

FitzRandolph
Observatory

Boiler House

Poe Field

Pardee Field

Caldwell
Field House

6

5

MacMillan

1912 Pavilion

Frelinghuysen
Field

Mass
Spectrometry
Lab

Chilled
Water
Plant

1895
Field

Bedford
Field

Gulick
Field

Washington Road

Armory

Architectural Lab

Elementary Particles Labs

Butler Apartments →

7

Cooling
Towers

Tennis
Courts

Jadwin Gymnasium

Elm Drive

Lake Carnegie

8

Pennsylvania Railroad

Faculty Road

To Route 1

Boathouse

Rowing Tank

9

E F G H J K L M

Appendix 1 Conservation of Outdoor Sculpture

Youngja Lee Kim

It is a common conception that outdoor sculpture is durable and everlasting. When Roman bronze statues have survived millenia, it is hard to conceive that modern bronze sculpture has serious problems. However, the use of new materials and technology combined with the increase in air pollution and vandalism have resulted in a multitude of problems for the conservation of outdoor sculpture. The John B. Putnam, Jr., Memorial Collection is no exception.

The materials used for sculptures in the Putnam Collection include bronze, painted mild and Cor-Ten steel, stainless steel, aluminum, concrete, granite, and marble. All but the marble sculpture have been sited outdoors for nearly ten years. The stainless steel, aluminum, and concrete sculptures have withstood the environment very well, showing no visual signs of weathering. However, all the bronze sculptures have corroded differently, depending on their location, quality of the casting, and their design. Cor-Ten steel corroded severely where there was retention of moisture. The painted mild steel sculptures have had to be repainted every few years due to paint loss and failure of the base metal.

In addition to the problem of corrosion, the Putnam sculptures have been subjected to vandalism. Often, outdoor sculpture is sat on, climbed on, written on, and in some cases broken off. Physical participation by the viewers is even encouraged by some artists. (When Henry Moore visited the Princeton campus, he was delighted to see a student cuddled on his sculpture reading.) Unfortunately, not all participations are harmless and amusing. Naum Gabo's *Spheric Theme* has thin spring wires that are constantly stretched and broken off. The bronze knife and rope of George Segal's *Abraham and Isaac* were broken off twice within half a year. Graffiti on *Oval with Points* was written with a black magic marker that permanently stained a part of the patina. A vandal painted a bright pink and green sign of arrows on the porous concrete surface of Pablo Picasso's *Head of a Woman*. Clement Meadmore's *Upstart II*, which originally had a rustic Cor-Ten surface, had

to be painted because of recurring problems with graffiti. Arnoldo Pomodoro's *Sphere VI* was hit with a metal tool leaving puncture holes, dents, and scratches.

The Art Museum has been maintaining the John B. Putnam, Jr., Memorial Collection since 1976. Major conservation work has been done on six of the sculptures: Jacques Lipchitz's *Song of the Vowels*, Louise Nevelson's *Atmosphere and Environment X*, Naum Gabo's *Spheric Theme*, Clement Meadmore's *Upstart II*, Tony Smith's *Moses*, and Alexander Calder's *Five Disks: One Empty*. The work involved lifting the sculpture, removing corrosion, and in some cases blast-cleaning and painting. Annual maintenance includes washing with a non-ironic detergent and applying a coating that is a mixture of carnauba and bees wax and lavender oil. The annual maintenance does appear to be slowing the weathering process, and with grants from the National Endowment for the Arts in Washington, D.C., and matching funds from the John B. Putnam, Jr., Memorial Fund, the Museum has been able to do research on the causes of corrosion to outdoor sculpture and to find remedies for treating it.

Bronze, which has been a favorite medium for traditional statuary as well as contemporary sculpture, is classified as a wrought or cast alloy. The wrought alloy can contain up to 95 percent copper and as much as 10 percent tin. The contemporary cast alloys, of which all Princeton's bronze sculptures are made, usually have a copper content of up to 80 percent, 10 percent tin, 25 percent lead, and some zinc.[1]

When bronze is exposed to the atmosphere, it usually forms a patina that is at first brown, then dull black, and eventually green. The length of time it takes to develop a green patina depends on the degree of pollution, humidity, and temperature.[2] However, the patina on sculptures in the Putnam Collection, as well as on most modern bronze sculptures, is achieved artificially at foundries by applying various chemicals to the surface of the cleaned

American Indian students at Princeton
with Moore sculpture

tion of the corrosion spots on the sculpture suggested that there was a connection between the corrosion and the chemicals sprayed on the lawn. Besides the minute particles of corrosion, there were small patches of pale green corrosion where the porocity existed due to improper venting while casting. The porous areas remain wet long after a rainfall and the rate of corrosion is usually much higher when relative humidity increases.[3] The green patches were removed by scraping with small hand tools and an abrasive. They were then degreased with acetone and repatinated with ferric nitrate to match the original brown. After washing the porous areas with a non-ironic detergent and allowing them to dry, they were sealed with a mixture of bees and carnauba waxes.

Reg Butler suggested that the patches of corrosion be removed with a brass wire brush, the porous areas be sealed with polyester resin, and the surface be "well loaded" with a wax polish.[4] A base to separate the sculpture from the lawn should be installed in the near future.

Gaston Lachaise's *Floating Figure* is the only bronze sculpture at Princeton that has been free of problems. The excellent condition of the sculpture probably is due to its minimum porocity and smooth surface, its siting, which is away from a heavily traveled street, and its high pedestal that protects the sculpture from possible contamination from lawn and soil as well as from vandalism.

Jacques Lipchitz's *Song of the Vowels*, which was patinated in black with ammonium sulfide, developed a subtle green untertone from weathering. Localized corrosion was severe where porocity of the metal existed and numerous pin holes existed from poor venting. Light green patches of corrosion were especially bad on both underarms and hands. In certain severely corroded areas, 3/8-inch white crystals and an uneven green patina were observed. From x-ray diffraction and chemical analysis, white crystals were identified as gypsum, a core material. The objectives of conservation for *Song of the Vowels* were first, to correct the cause of uneven corrosion and second, to slow down the rate of deterioration.

metal. Artists usually specify the color of patina and sometimes work closely with the foundry while patinating their works.

Reg Butler's *The Bride* developed minute blue-white particles of corrosion on the part of the sculpture nearest the ground that were not found on other sculptures in the collection. *The Bride* was installed directly on the ground with no space between it and the lawn, which had been fertilized and chemically sprayed. The shape, pattern, and loca-

The treatment, given in 1976, consisted of removing the corrosion with hand tools and an abrasive, re-patinating the affected areas, filling pinholes and cracks, and coating the entire sculpture with the mixture of waxes and oil. In order to decrease the condensation of moisture on the metal surface and to aerate the inside, the sculpture was placed one inch above the platform. Since this major restoration, *Song of the Vowels* has not had corrosion problems.[5]

Due to frequent touching and sitting, Henry Moore's *Oval with Points* had lost a considerable amount of the original green patina on the lower part of the opening. However, the bronze is in a stable condition and the area blends in rather well with the rest of the sculpture. A color contrast had also developed between the tree-shaded and non-shaded section of the sculpture. It was thought that the contrast resulted from the tree sap that was being deposited on the shaded area. The tree became infected and had to be cut down. Since then, the uneven change in the patina has been arrested and the sculture has required far less maintenance. Both changes in *Oval with Points* appear to be limited to the patina only. There is no visual sign of corrosion of the bronze itself, probably due to its minimum porosity.

On Arnaldo Pomodoro's *Sphere VI*, the areas that are in sunken relief are corroding faster than the smoothly polished areas. The patina on the reliefs is greener, especially where rain water is trapped. Also, the patina on the lower-most part facing the ground has been changing to green faster. There are many small holes through which a considerable amount of water gets inside. We have recommended that *Sphere VI* be placed indoors. Pomodoro prefers *Sphere VI* to be polished and varnished.[6]

George Segal's *Abraham and Isaac*, which was patinated in black, developed numerous white spots one week after its arrival from the foundry. It was so disfigured that the founder had to immediately repatinate most of the base and some areas on the two figures. With Segal's permission, a wax coating was applied in order to prevent corrosion. However, Segal later felt that the wax coating, which was glossy, was too decorative and polished for his sculpture, and that the glossy surface tended to destroy the raw dramatic conflict he wished to convey. He requested that the sculpture be stripped of wax and allowed to weather naturally to see if time would produce the rich, multi-hued patina that he admired on an old Rodin sculpture at the Johnson estate in Princeton.[7]

Cor-Ten steel is a high-strength, low-alloy steel, commonly known to be durable, self-sealing, and corrosion-resistant, and, therefore, maintenance free. It is favored by artists for its rich, rustic color that progresses from shades of orange, russet, and brown to a final cinnamon or bluish cinnamon. Nevertheless, because the colors on Cor-Ten steel progress, if Cor-Ten becomes scratched, these areas take a very long time to match the color that has developed on the rest of the area. Any scratches or marks with paint are relatively permanent. On surfaces exposed to the atmosphere, a dense and tightly adherent protective oxide coating is supposed to develop, protecting the metal from further corrosion. However, the performance of Cor-Ten as a corrosion-resistant material depends heavily on the design and fabrication of a particular sculpture and its environment. When the surface of Cor-Ten steel is continually wet, it corrodes at an unacceptably high rate. Pockets, crevices, and faying surfaces that will collect moisture should be avoided in the design. It is necessary that the manufacturer's recommendations for Cor-Ten be strictly adhered to in designing, fabricating, and choosing a site for a Cor-Ten steel sculpture.[8]

Clement Meadmore's *Upstart II* and Louise Nevelson's *Atmosphere and Environment X* are both fabricated of Cor-Ten steel. Originally, both had the rustic Cor-Ten surface. But they were painted later because of excessive corrosion and problems with graffiti. Clement Meadmore's *Upstart II* was painted a flat charcoal gray before the Museum was in charge of maintaining the collection. Although the paint protected the metal from corroding in most parts of the sculpture, the joint in the middle where the two main components met was corroded severly. The interstice at the joint collected moisture that oozed out from the inside and retained the moisture that was condensed. When the sculpture was disassembled, loose piles of rust were found on several areas because the interior surface had not been protected. The primary causes or corrosion were probably moisture retention at the joint and high humidity inside the sculpture.

Upstart II was disassembled into its two primary components and taken to Lippincott, Inc., the original fabricator of the sculpture. The conservation job prescribed by The Art Museum was followed. The treatment given included sandblasting both interior and exterior surfaces to clean the rust, replacing the severely corroded steel plate near the joint, welding the joint to prevent retention of moisture, coating the inside with Ziebart rust proofing sealant to minimize corrosion inside, and priming and painting the exterior surface.

Although welding the joints changed the number of main components and the nature of the joint, the extent of the corrosion at the joint and the surrounding area was so severe that the alternative of placing a gasket would not have been as permanent a solution to corrosion as welding. When Clement Meadmore was consulted about welding the joint, he told us that he specified the number and position of the joints mainly to facilitate transportation and that he tried to have the fewest joints possible, and these where they would be unobtrusive and fairly neutral. He was in complete agreement with the procedures that were specified, including welding.[9] Even though *Upstart II* did not meet the height clearance for turnpikes after the two sections were welded together, it was possible to transport it from North Haven, Connecticut, to Princeton, New Jersey, by means of local roads.

Louise Nevelson's *Environment and Atmosphere X* had developed severe corrosion on most of the horizontal joints between the boxes that make up the sculpture. Corrosion on the base was widely disseminated and severe. The more severely corroded surfaces were porous and granular in texture. The corrosion process was not self-sealing, as expected from Cor-Ten steel, and was progressing rapidly.

A series of analyses on corroded samples of Cor-Ten and on the shim material was carried out using an Auger electron spectroscopy, x-ray fluorescence, and optical microscopy. Based on the results of these tests and on a visual observation,[10] the primary cause of the corrosion appeared to be moisture retention caused by a design that is not suitable for Cor-Ten steel. Although the higher carbon content of the shim material and its higher rate of corrosion indicate that an alloy other than Cor-Ten was probably used for shimming, galvanic corrosion had been eliminated as a possible cause of deterioration because of the absence of any elements that can cause galvanic corrosion in low-alloy steels. It is known, however, that even the coupling of steels containing different amounts of carbon and alloy elements can cause a galvanic effect. But any definite conclusions about the possibility of galvanic corrosion were difficult to draw from the data obtained.

The treatment that was given at Lippincott, Inc., the original fabricator of *Environment and Atmosphere X*, consisted of disassembling the entire piece into its unit components, removing the corrosion products, and priming and painting the entire sculpture, including facing surfaces. The Art Museum wanted to save the original Cor-Ten surface, but Louise Nevelson decided to have *Atmosphere and Environment X* painted in flat black.[11]

Mild steel is a carbon steel—lighter in weight with a higher rate of corrosion than Cor-Ten steel. Mild steel is rarely used without a protective coating when the surface is to be exposed to the environment. Almost invariably, a sculpture made of mild steel is painted or galvanized. It has to be protected by priming, painting, galvanizing, or a cathodic protection. For mild steel buried underground, cathodic protection as well as priming and painting is recommended. Performance of the paint depends on proper preparation of the base metal, compatibility of the primer with the base metal, quality of the paint, and the environment to which it is exposed.[12]

In painting steel sculptures, aesthetic considerations are equally as important as the durability of the paint used to protect the steel underneath. The color and glossiness of a sculpture that is selected should match those of the original paint that the artist specified. Although a new coat of paint can be applied over the existing paint layer when the problems are limited to local areas, the new coat would not last long if the primer has failed and the base metal is corroded. Furthermore, when several layers of paint have been applied, the steel loses its characteristic hard steel-like appearance. The edges, nuts, and bolts lose their clarity and tend to look rather plastic.

Five Disks: One Empty was fabricated with ½ -inch mild steel plates joined both by welding and by using nuts and bolts. The four feet of the sculpture were mounted on rectangular copper-covered bases that were filled with concrete when it was installed in 1970. *Five Disks: One Empty* was later repainted with a flat charcoal gray over the original flat black. The bond between the original paint and the new one was poor, and both coats of paint peeled. Corrosion developed at the joints where one steel plate overlapped the other and on the four feet. The rust on the feet was accelerated by the copper bases, which might have caused galvanic corrosion.

To restore the original flat black and to prevent further rusting, *Five Disks: One Empty* was sandblasted, coated with a durable epoxy primer, and painted with Glidden's flat black paint, which was the same paint used by the artist.

In the future, the bases, which can easily be mistaken as an integral part of the sculpture itself, should be removed to prevent corrosion and the joints around the faying surfaces, especially the upper ones, should be sealed. Priming and painting all the faying surfaces to prevent rust problems between them would be more permanent than sealing the joints. However, treating the faying surfaces would mean disassembling the sculpture, which would involve enormously difficult work even for the fabricator who specializes in large-scale sculptures.

Tony Smith's *Moses* is made of galvanized mild steel, which is steel coated with zinc. It was originally finished with a coating of linseed oil. Serious rust problems developed where the zinc and linseed oil coatings failed. Galvanized steel protects ferrous metal because the zinc, which is anodic to iron, is sacrificially corroded when moisture penetrates the base metal. Because both the zinc and linseed oil coatings failed to respond to local treatment, it was sandblasted, primed with a zinc-rich primer, and painted with Benjamin Moore's risisto umber black, which was recommended and approved by Tony Smith.[13]

The surrounding lawn, which is level with the base of *Moses*, lies lower than the rest of the ground nearby. When it rains, puddles of water surround the sculpture. When funds are available, the part of the sculpture that becomes immersed in the water should be given cathodic protection as well as a coat of primer and paint to prevent serious corrosion and damage and eventual structural instability.

Stainless steels, which meet the demands for physical strength and for resistance to corrosion, chemical attack, and heat, are basically alloys of chromium, nickel, and iron. Their corrosion resistance is due to the presence of at least 12 percent chromium. The addition of nickel enables better corrosion resistance. The most common steel in this group contains 18 percent chromium and 8 percent nickel, often indicated by the number 18–8.[14]

Naum Gabo's *Spheric Theme*, George Rickey's *Two Planes Vertical Horizontal II*, and Kenneth Snelson's *Northwood II* are the stainless-steel sculptures in the Putnam Collection. None of them show any signs of atmospheric corrrosion, but there are mechanical failures of Naum Gabo's *Spheric Theme* due to the nature of its design.

Naum Gabo's *Spheric Theme* is fabricated of 1/8 inch-thick stainless steel plates and two different gauges of spring wires which were constantly stretched and broken off. Most of the damaged wires were the thinner wires probably because the thinner ones are more easily stretched than the thicker wires. The welding failed at one of the spots where the star-shaped center piece met the outer circular plate. The failure was probably caused by the vibration of the wide circular plate. Any pressure on one part of the plate creates a resonance (reverberation) for the entire plate. The paint on the star-shaped part peeled off due to its poor adhesion to the steel and lifted from the metal like a piece of paper.

Spheric Theme was moved inside for repairs. All of the thin wires were replaced with heavy wires, which are harder to stretch and break off. The repair work for the failed weld spot and the peeled paint were postponed because an ideal indoor site to protect the sculpture from vandalism and wind was not available. Recently, however, the decision was made to place the sculpture in the courtyard of the Engineering Quadrangle, which will give it partial protection from the wind. The unfinished repair work including painting and welding are in progress.

Aluminum is a light metal that welds well and machines satisfactorily. Although aluminum is a less noble metal, which means in scientific terms occupying a low place in the Potential Series, it has quite high resistance to water and atmospheric corrosion due to the formation of a protective film of aluminum oxide of various thicknesses. However, when aluminum is in contact with more noble metals such as copper and iron, corrosion of aluminum is enhanced.[15]

Eduardo Paolozzi's *Marok-Marok-Miosa* is the only sculpture in the Putnam Collection that is made entirely of aluminum. It has had no problems with corrosion due to its indoor location and aluminum's resistance to corrosion.

Michael Hall's *Mastodon VI* is made of bronze and aluminum. Although there is no sign of corrosion on the aluminum part that is in contact with the copper, there is a possibility that this contact could cause corrosion of the aluminum in the future.

Isamu Noguchi's *White Sun*, which is made of marble, and Masayuki Nagare's *Stone Riddle*, which is made of granite, have had no conservation problems. Marble is vulnerable when subjected to acidic rains, atmospheric pollutants, and freezing and thawing cycles. Granite, an igneous rock, is very durable and resistant to weathering. However, pollution and frequent freezing and thawing can accelerate its rate of weathering.[16]

It is a common practice to deal with the conservation of outdoor sculpture only after a sculpture begins to have conservation problems. This oversight can lead eventually to refabrication, which can be very costly.

It cannot be emphasized enough that the conservation of outdoor sculpture should begin with a proper design for the selected medium, followed by thoughtful fabrication, installation, and regularly scheduled preventative maintenance. Furthermore, the experience with the Putnam Collection has shown that the design, fabrication, and installation of the sculptures must be done with consideration given to their interaction with the environment. The preservation and maintenance of outdoor sculpture depends on all of these conservation efforts to be successful and effective.

Carl Nesjar cleaning mold
for Picasso's *Head of a Woman*

Born in Larvik, Norway, in 1920, Carl Nesjar spent part of his childhood and youth in the United States. His professional training took place at Pratt Institute and Columbia University in New York City, and at the National School of Arts and Crafts and the Royal Academy of Art in Oslo. Later, in Paris, he studied printmaking with Stanley W. Hayter at Atelier 17, and lithography with Jean Pons. Represented in numerous public and private collections in Norway and Sweden with murals, wall hangings, concrete and steel sculptural reliefs, paintings, prints, and photographs, Nesjar is also a familiar figure in Scandinavia for his theater designs, and for his documentary and experimental films.

Nesjar's long and fruitful association with Picasso began in early 1957 when he showed Picasso photographs of his experiments with *Naturbetong*, a process of making concrete with a prepacked aggregate that would then be partially exposed through sandblasting. This process had recently been developed by Nesjar's Oslo friends, the architect Erling Viksjö

and the engineer Sverre Jystad. The potential of the medium quickly captured the imagination of the seventy-five-year-old master. He found in the process a means of construction for the monumental works he had envisioned in creating his sculpture maquettes—and saw in Nesjar the potential collaborator for their execution. Accordingly, Picasso gave the Norwegian artist three unsigned drawings for trial translation into engraved-concrete murals for the new government building in Oslo designed by Viksjö. So successful was this 1957 experiment that Picasso later sanctioned the execution of the first, 10-foot-high, experimental construction based on one of his maquettes; it was erected in 1958 in the village of Gon near Nesjar's birthplace of Larvik. Subsequently twenty works, located in Norway, Sweden, the Netherlands, France, Spain, Israel, and the United States, resulted from the collaboration between Picasso and Nesjar before Picasso's death in 1973. Two outdoor engraved friezes realized from drawings by Picasso are among the more imposing. The first, executed in 1960–1961 on the three sides of the Colegio de los Arquitectos in Barcelona, totals 260 feet in length; within the building, are two additional murals, each approximately 10 by 35 feet. The second frieze, 80 feet long, was executed in 1963 on Douglas Cooper's estate at Château de Castille (Argilliers), near the Pont du Gard in Provence. Realizations of sculpture maquettes by Picasso include *Woman with Outstretched Arms*, completed in 1962 for the garden of Daniel-Henri Kahnweiler at Chalo-St. Mars near Etampes, south of Paris; a giant *Head of a Woman* (1964), 15 meters high, for the town of Kristinehamn on Lake Vänern, Sweden; a *Déjeuner sur l'Herbe*, consisting of four figures between 3 to 4 meters high, for the grounds of the Museum of Modern Art in Stockholm (1965–1966); and the 38-foot-high *Bust of Sylvette* (1968), piquantly holding court for the occupants of the surrounding 30-story apartment complex in University Plaza, designed for New York University by I.M. Pei.[1] All these pre-date Princeton's *Head of a Woman*, which Nesjar characterized on its comple-

Nesjar sandblasting *Head* for definition of drawing and color

tion in 1971 as having "what the French call *de la gueule*," namely "character"—or more colloquially, "oomph." In 1975, Nesjar completed a 28-foot-high sculpture, popularly called "The Bather," from one of Picasso's maquettes, for the semi-public grounds surrounding the central offices and research facilities of Gould, Inc., an electronics firm near Chicago.

Throughout his collaboration with Picasso, Nesjar remained engaged in his own projects. Chief among them in recent years has been the search for an effective means of combining and exploiting the brilliant but ephemeral physical attributes of natural ice and water formations in combination with properties of light and his own sculptural designs. Terming these works all-year or ice fountains, Nesjar says of them: "In the cold Scandinavian climate ordinary fountains have to be shut down nearly half of the year because of the cold. I have found a way to keep fountains flowing all year round and to let the ice that forms on them become a series of constantly changing shapes and patterns throughout the winter."[2] Nesjar has created ice fountains in Norway, in the French Alps (at Flaine, the sports and cultural complex designed by Marcel Breuer), and, most recently, at Lake Placid, in connection with the Winter Olympics of 1980. In 1973–1974, he was a research fellow of the Center for Advanced Visual Studies at the Massachusetts Institute of Technology, Cambridge, and continued to work there intermittently as a guest of the center until 1980.

Notes

Introduction

1. H. H. Arnason, *History of Modern Art*, p. 60.
2. Umberto Boccioni, "Technical Manifesto of Futurist Sculpture," in Robert Herbert, *Modern Artists on Art*, p. 56.
3. George Rickey, in Michael Blackwood, *The History of Modern Sculpture*, part 3 of a film, 1979.

1 Reg Butler

1. Louisville, Kentucky, 1963, *Reg Butler: A Retrospective Exhibition*, exh. cat., no. 94.
2. Letter to the author, October 8, 1975.
3. New York, 1962, *Reg Butler: Recent Sculpture (1959–1962)*, exh. cat., n. pag.
4. The maquette was wantonly shattered by a disturbed refugee while on exhibition with other prize-winning models at the Tate Gallery in 1953. Two additional preliminary bronze models of 1952 and a subsequent bronze working model made in 1957 for the Brussels World's Fair appeared in Butler's retrospective exhibition in Louisville in 1963. A variant maquette is in the collection of The Museum of Modern Art in New York and several preliminary drawings belong to the Carnegie/Mellon Institute in Pittsburgh.
5. Robert Goldwater, *What Is Modern Sculpture?*, p. 127. The variant maquette owned by The Museum of Modern Art (see note 4) is illustrated on p. 124.
6. Butler's small daughter, associating the sculptures with churches and steeples, haltingly called them "tcheekles," a designation the artist considered "as good a name as any." Letter to the author, May 12, 1976.
7. *Reg Butler: Recent Sculpture (1959–1962)*, n. pag.
8. Letter to the author, May 12, 1976.
9. The remaining bronzes, whose order of strike is undetermined, are in the collections of the city of Louisville, Kentucky (the gift of Mrs. Dann C. Byck, Sr.); Mrs. Percy Uris, Palm Beach, Florida; and the Pierre Matisse Gallery, New York City.

2 Alexander Calder

1. It was Jean Arp in the early 1930s who dubbed Calder's stationary sculptures "stabiles," and Marcel Duchamp who coined the term "mobiles" for the constructions that moved.
2. For a fuller discussion of Calder's technical methods, see Jean Lipman, *Calder's Universe*, pp. 305–310.
3. Confirmed by Calder in a conversation with the author, October 1975.

4. Lipman, *Calder's Universe*, p. 306. Robert Osborn, in "Calder's International Monuments," p. 49, aptly observes that this ribbing and bracing (as well as the patterned sequences created by the square-headed bolts) add their own aesthetic to the sculpture.
5. Letter to Alfred Barr, March 18, 1969. Calder was preoccupied with several projects, including a large stabile for Grand Rapids, Michigan (*La Grande Vitesse*), and a major retrospective exhibition for the Fondation Maeght at Saint-Paul-de-Vence, for which he made another monumental stabile (*Morning Cobweb*).
6. Letter to the author, June 26, 1969.
7. Letter to Alfred Barr, March 7, 1970.
8. Letter to Alfred Barr, March 28, 1970.

3 Sir Jacob Epstein

1. Jacob Epstein, *Let There Be Sculpture*, pp. 67–68.
2. Ibid.
3. Ibid., p. 69. In addition to the Tate Gallery and Putnam Memorial strikes, other casts known to the author exist in the Birmingham Museums and Art Gallery; the Fitzwilliam Museum, Cambridge; St. Catherine's College, Oxford; the Yale University Art Gallery; and the Institute for Advanced Study in Princeton.
4. *Modern British Drawings, Paintings and Sculpture*, Christie's, London, October 30, 1970, no. 231. Mrs. Yates died in 1973. Mr. E. A. Bright, an adviser who arranged the sale of the Einstein bust for Mrs. Yates at Christie's, has informed me that the bust was purchased by Mrs. Yates's husband, Charles Peel Yates, sometime before 1950 from a collector or art dealer in Southport, Lancashire, who was at the time in possession of a number of Epstein sculptures.
5. It was shown in the exhibition "Twentieth Century Portraits," held at The Museum of Modern Art, New York, in 1942. The bust is now in the faculty dining room at the Institute. Dr. Carl Kaysen, former director of the Institute for Advanced Study, generously provided the author with documentary information and other helpful material on this version of the sculpture.

4 Naum Gabo

1. Antoine Pevsner's sculpture is also represented in the Putnam Memorial (*Construction in the Third and Fourth Dimension*).
2. Lecture at Princeton University, April 22, 1975.
3. Robert Goldwater, *What is Modern Sculpture?*, The Museum of Modern Art, New York, 1969, p. 67.

4. *The Daily Princetonian*, interview with Christopher Farrill, Februay 22, 1975.

5. Naum Gabo, *Gabo*, unnumbered page facing plate 64.

5 Michael David Hall

1. Vanderbilt University Gallery, Nashville, Tennessee, 1968, *Mastodon: Recent Sculpture by Michael Hall*, exh. cat., n. pag.

2. Clara Hieronymus, "Old Gym's New Mastodons," pp. D–1, 3.

3. Vanderbilt University Gallery, Nashville, Tennessee, 1968, *Mastodon: Recent Sculpture by Michael Hall*, exh. cat., n. pag.

4. Wright State University Art Gallery, Dayton, Ohio, 1974, *Michael Hall: El Tiburon*, exh. cat., n. pag.

6 Gaston Lachaise

1. Gerald Nordland, *Gaston Lachaise*, p. 21. French's *Christian Student* once graced the Princeton campus until undergraduate protest forced its banishment in 1931.

2. Joseph Brummer, a scholarly dealer specializing in antiquities, medieval, and Renaissance art, was a onetime pupil of Rodin and had a particular affection for sculpture. This, together with a strong inclination to further the cause of modern art, led him to present the first one-man exhibitions in America of Maillol, Despiau, Brancusi, and Lipchitz.

3. Nordland, *Lachaise*, pp. 131, 133. *Floating Figure* had evolved from three earlier variations on the theme: *Dusk*, a small bas-relief of 1917; and two states of a truncated *Floating Figure*, executed in 1924 and related more closely to the final version of 1927 (ibid., p. 130).

4. Dorothy C. Miller, in a letter to the author, April 12, 1976, recalls the occasion as follows: "Lachaise supervised the first cast of *Floating Figure* for the Lachaise exhibition held January 28–March 5, 1935 at the MOMA. The sculpture was returned to his studio at the close of the exhibition and was subsequently presented to the Museum in his memory in February 1937. The then 'anonymous donors' were those gentlemen who had helped Lachaise so generously for so many years, Philip L. Goodwin, George L. K. Morris, Edward M. M. Warburg, and Lincoln Kirstein. My memory is of the delivery of the bronze by the founder just before the Lachaise exhibition opened. Alfred Barr had prepared a high pedestal for it which was waiting on the second (parlor) floor of the town house where the ceiling was high enough to accommodate it. I remember the terrific excitement we all felt as the heavy figure (840 pounds) was hauled up the staircase and hoisted with difficulty on to the pedestal. It was too big for the tiny elevator."

5. The handsome pentagonal granite pedestal, which enhances the illusion of levitation of Princeton's *Floating Figure*, was designed by the late Michael Rapuano, consultant landscape architect to the University from 1961 to 1973.

7 Jacques Lipchitz

1. In the collections of the Musée d'Art Moderne de la Ville de Paris; Cornell University; Nelson A. Rockefeller Estate, Pocantico Hills, New York; the University of California at Los Angeles; and the Kröller-Müller Museum, Otterlo, The Netherlands.

2. H. H. Arnason, *Jacques Lipchitz: Sketches in Bronze*, fig. 69, p. 103. In the later 1960s, Lipchitz cast approximately 150 of his surviving sketches for sculptures into bronze to preserve a record of his "first inspiration and encounters." That *Song of the Vowels* differs from the original clay maquette in the Museum of Modern Art by having a square plinth. Arnason's first publication of these small bronzes in 1969 roughly coincided with the casting of the final, large-scale version of the sculpture by Lipchitz himself for Princeton. It appears likely, therefore, that the modification made sometime in the 1960s on the maquette (perhaps to provide greater stability) influenced the subsequent casting of the Princeton bronze.

3. "Eleven Europeans in America," interviews with James Johnson Sweeney, *The Museum of Modern Art Bulletin*, XIII, Nos. 4–5 (1946), 24–26.

4. A. M. Hammacher, *Jacques Lipchitz: His Sculpture*, p. 48.

5. Sweeney, "Eleven Europeans," p. 26.

6. From the archives of the collections of The Museum of Modern Art, New York.

7. Jacques Lipchitz, *My Life in Sculpture*, p. 123.

8 Clement Meadmore

1. Hilton Kramer, "'Less is More': A Minimal Touch," *New York Times*, April 29, 1977, p. C20.

2. Jeanne Siegel, "Clement Meadmore: Circling the Square," p. 56.

3. Undated letter to the author, probably in March, 1975.

4. Siegel, "Circling the Square," p. 65.

5. Grand Rapids, Michigan, 1973, *Sculpture off the Pedestal*, exh. cat., n. pag.

6. Undated letter to the author (March 1975), *Upstart I*, the first of this series, is in the collection of Mrs. Harry Lynde Bradley of Milwaukee, Wisconsin. It previously had figured prominently in the 1967 outdoor exhibition "Sculpture in the Environment," in which a number of monumental sculptures were placed in public locations throughout New York City.

7. Hugh M. Davies, "Clement Meadmore," p. 7.

9 Henry Moore

1. Letter to the author questioning Moore, April 21, 1969, from Wildenstein & Co., Inc.

2. London, 1968, *Henry Moore*, exh. cat., pp. 53–55.

3. This and the following quotation are from Julian Huxley, *Memories*, II (New York: Harper and Row, 1973), 253–254. A photograph of the Huxleys with their elephant skull appears among the illustrations following p. 128.

4. An album of thirty-two etchings, printed in Paris under the direction of Jacques Frélant, was issued in a limited edition of 115 copies by Gérald Cramer, Geneva, in 1970. After Moore received the skull, he "did not work on it right away . . . . There it sat like some ancient totem slowly and surely making its presence felt" (Geneva, 1970–1971, *Elephant Skull*, exh. cat. n. pag.).

5. The second strike figured prominently in the massive retrospective exhibition of the sculptor's work held in the summer of 1972 at the Forte di Belvedere, overlooking Florence. The largest permanent holdings of Moore's sculptures are now in London (Tate Gallery), Toronto (Art Gallery), and Washington, D.C. (Hirshhorn Museum and Sculpture Garden).

10 Masayuki Nagare

1. New York, 1965, *Recent Sculpture of Masayuki Nagare*, exh. cat., n. pag.

2. I should like to express my appreciation to Mr. George Staempfli and Mr. Phillips A. Bruno of the Staempfli Gallery for their generous assistance in providing exhibition catalogues (1963, 1965, 1967–1968, 1973), chronologies, and other supporting information for this essay. Their cooperation was the more important since no full-length studies of the artist exist to date.

3. The construction was re-erected after the Fair, in a revised design by Nagare, at Manhattan College, Purchase, New York.

4. Among the few works by Nagare to be based on a specific object, *Bachi* derives from the traditional shape of the carved ivory *bachi* or pick employed by geishas in plucking the strings of the guitarlike *samisen*.

5. *Recent Sculpture of Masayuki Nagare*, n. pag.

6. The landscaping for this interior court, which is also the site of Dimitri Hadzi's bronze sculpture, *Thermopylae* (see Checklist), was designed by the late Michael Rapuano, consultant landscape architect to Princeton University.

7. Presented to The Art Museum by Nancy R. Patton in memory of her father, Hugh McElveen Patton, Class of 1932.

11 Louise Nevelson

1. Otterlo, The Netherlands, 1969, *Louise Nevelson: Sculpture 1959–1969*, exh. cat. n. pag. See also Colette Roberts, *Nevelson*, p. 13.

2. Nevelson twice visited Mexico in 1950 and the art of its ancient cultures made a profound impression on her. "This was a world of form that at once I felt was mine, a world where East and West met, a world of geometry and magic." (Roberts, *Nevelson*, p. 16).

3. Minneapolis, 1973, *Nevelson: Wood Sculptures*, exh. cat., no. 49, p. 7.

4. Revealing parallels can be drawn from a comparison between the sixth-century mosaic depicting the Palace of Theodoric in Sant 'Apollinare Nuovo in Ravenna and Nevelson's *Night Focus Dawn* of 1969 in The Whitney Museum of American Art; compare André Grabar, *Byzantine Painting* (Geneva: Editions Albert Skira, 1953), p. 56, and *Nevelson: Wood Sculptures*, p. 56.

5. An architectural screen employed to shield the mystery of the Mass from the congregation in churches of the Eastern rite.

6. Although the elaborate golden altar in the basilica of San Marco in Venice possesses an overlay design encrusted with Byzantine enamels and precious stones, less richly decorated frontals (*pala d'altare*), constructed of rare or polychromed woods, were more common throughout the Latin West.

7. Louise Nevelson, *Dawns and Dusks*.

8. Ibid., p. 171.

9. *Nevelson: Wood Sculptures*, p. 31.

12 Isamu Noguchi

1. An interview with the sculptor by John Gruen and a picture survey by Ruth Wolfe in *Art in America*, March-April 1968, pp. 28–45, give an excellent account of Noguchi's career to that date.

2. The Art Museum, Princeton University, is fortunate to possess a number of paintings by Ch'i Pai-shih in its collection of Far Eastern art.

3. Letter to the author, September 4, 1975.

13 Eduardo Paolozzi

1. He produced a number of metal constructions, both accomplished and individual, that were exhibited at the Galerie Maeght and at Réalitées Nouvelles.

2. Dubuffet had formed a collection of coarse and perverse creations of untrained, naïve, and insane "artists," which he exhibited in Paris in 1949 as *art brut*.

3. These include a fountain and a sculpture for the Festival of Britain and three outdoor fountains for a park in Hamburg, Germany.

4. For a fuller account of Paolozzi's ties with the Independent Group, see Uwe M. Schneede, *Eduardo Paolozzi*, pp. 5–9. Schneede's concise account of the artist's unique career is recommended for further reading as well as for illustrations of his sculptures.

5. Richard Hamilton's diverting collage of 1956, *Just What Is It That Makes Today's Home So Different, So Appealing?*, is considered to be the first pictorial representation created in pop art. Composed of cutout elements from American magazines, it depicts a middle-class interior furnished with tasteless furniture and decor, and occupied by a male and a female nude. The "Atlas-body-built" male clutches a lollipop labelled "POP," a term coined in 1954 by the English art critic Lawrence Alloway to categorize the themes of popular culture.

6. Jasia Reichardt, "Eduardo Paolozzi," p. 155. The drawing is illustrated in Schneede, *Paolozzi*, p. 5.

7. London, 1971, *Eduardo Paolozzi*, exh. cat., p. 5.

8. Christopher Finch, "Paolozzi in the Sixties," p. 26. Finch relates: "Much of this material is classified according to Paolozzi's own system. There is for instance a silver scrap book covering everything from chrome bumpers to silver clothes."

9. Ibid., p. 27.

10. By 1960, Paolozzi had been represented in one-man or in group exhibitions in London, New York City, Venice, Sao Paōlo, Arnhem, Antwerp, Kassel, Tokyo, and Paris.

11. The others are *Rizla* (Tate Gallery, London) and *Akapotik Rose* (Nelson A. Rockefeller Estate, Pocantico Hills, New York). For illustrations of these, and of *Crash* (Ulster Museum, Belfast) and *Medea* (Rijksmuseum Kröller-Müller, Otterlo), see Finch, "Paolozzi in the Sixties," pp. 29 and 31.

14 Antoine Pevsner

1. Gabo is also represented in the Putnam Memorial Collection (*Spheric Theme*).

2. These bronzes are in the collections of the Musée National d'Art Moderne (Beaubourg), Paris (no. 1/3); the Thyssen Collection, Lugano, Switzerland (no. 2/3); and the Bezalel National Museum, Jerusalem (no. 3/3).

3. Dr. Marcel Joray has informed me in a letter that Giacometti and Jean Arp attended Mme Pevsner on the occasion of the casting of the first strike.

4. The family name was Pevsner. While in Norway with his brother in 1915, Naum began to sign his first constructions with the name Gabo.

5. To compensate for the increase in scale of the enlarged version of *Construction in the Third and Fourth Dimension*, Pevsner reduced the number of striations found on the smaller, earlier version and broadened the intervening surfaces.

6. Carola Giedion-Welcker, "Antoine Pevsner's spatial imagination," in Pierre Peissi, *Antoine Pevsner: Tribute by a Friend*, pp. 7–8.

7. The elegant lettering for the memorial was designed by the typographer P. J. Conkwright.

15 Pablo Picasso

1. New York, 1967, *The Sculpture of Picasso*, exh. cat., no. 151, p. 34.

2. The sculpture was first published by Hélène Parmelin, *Picasso—Women (1954–1963): Cannes and Mougins*, p. 87, col. repr.

3. *Sculpture of Picasso*, pp. 31–32.

4. For an account of Carl Nesjar and his collaboration with Picasso, see the Appendix 2.

5. *Sculpture of Picasso*, illus. p. 182.

6. "Bon à tirer," literally "good to print," is the standard French formula which, accompanied by the client's signature, signifies approval of a press sheet. This document is in the collection of The Art Museum. Undoubtedly recognizing that the combined costs of both artist's fee and construction expenses would be prohibitive, Picasso

neither asked for nor received compensation for the execution of *Head of a Woman*.

7. *Naturbetong* is a Norwegian word meaning "nature-concrete;" it was coined by Erling Viksjö, one of the two originators of the technique, in the belief that the results of this man-made process most closely resembled natural conglomerates, that is, fragments of stone embedded in sedimentary deposits.

8. Since the maquette, as part of Picasso's complex estate, has not been available for examination, this description is based on the color reproduction in Parmelin's *Picasso*, p. 87, and on Carl Nesjar's recollections of the original.

9. Efforts—so far unsuccessful—have been made to acquire the maquette of *Head of a Woman* for Princeton, in accordance with the hopes of the donor that original drawings and models of the Putnam sculptures could be obtained for educational purposes. The artist's reluctance to dispose of his unique sculptures has been pointed out previously. According to Nesjar, Picasso had parted with none of the approximately twenty maquettes realized in monumental concrete versions. His gift to the Art Institute of Chicago of the model for the sixty-foot-high *Woman's Head*, erected in sheet steel in Chicago's Civic Center in the late 1960s, seems to have been a rare instance of generosity.

Picasso was noncommittal about parting with the maquette when Nesjar first obtained his authorization for the Princeton sculpture in 1969, and it was decided to await completion of the latter before raising the question again. Early in April 1973, Nesjar was scheduled for an appointment with Picasso to review, among other business, the results of the Princeton project and to explore once again the possibility of his releasing the maquette; but Picasso's sudden death on April 8, 1973, intervened before the meeting could take place.

It is to be hoped that, once the complex problems of the artist's estate are fully resolved, efforts to acquire this small masterwork for Princeton will be resumed.

16 Arnaldo Pomodoro

1. Milan, 1974, *Arnaldo Pomodoro*, exh. cat., n. pag.
2. Ibid., n. pag.
3. Pesaro, Italy, 1971, *Arnaldo Pomodoro: Sculture nella città*, exh. cat., p. 7.
4. See Milan, 1974, *Pomodoro*, Hunter interview, n. pag.

5. Ibid., from which the dates cited in this paragraph are also taken.
6. London, 1968, *Arnaldo Pomodoro*, exh. cat., n. pag.
7. Ibid., n. pag.
8. Mila Pistoi, "Interview with Arnaldo Pomodoro," *Marcatre* (Milan), nos. 8–10, 1965, p. 240.
9. Pesaro, Italy, 1971, *Pomodoro*, p. 10.
10. The bronze is the first of three authorized strikes. A second has been made for a private collector in Brussels and the third has not yet been cast. Since the early 1960s, the majority of Pomodoro's sculptures have been cast by the foundries of Battaglia and De Andreis in Milan and of G. B. Esse in Verona.
11. Milan, 1974, *Pomodoro*, Hunter interview, n. pag.

17 George Rickey

1. Washington, D.C., 1966, *George Rickey: Sixteen Years of Kinetic Sculpture*, exh. cat., n. pag.
2. Naum Gabo, *Gabo*, p. 152.
3. Ibid., p. 160; the now famous interview was conducted by the sculptor Ibram Lassaw and the painter Ilya Bolotowsky.
4. The others are owned by Yale University; the city of Gelsenkirchen, Germany; the Santa Barbara Museum; and the Storm King Art Center, Mountainville, New York. *Two Planes Vertical Horizontal II* was exhibited at The Whitney Museum of American Art in 1970, and in the International Biennial Exhibition of Outdoor Sculpture at the Middleheim Museum in Antwerp in 1971.

18 George Segal

1. Louis Zona, "A Segal Comes to Youngstown," *Dialogue: The Ohio Arts Journal*, July/August 1980, p. 13.
2. Jan Van Der Marck, *George Segal*, p. 60.
3. John Coplans, "George Segal: An Interview," *Dialogue: The Ohio Arts Journal*, March/April 1980, p. 4.
4. Minneapolis, Walker Art Center, 1978, *George Segal: Sculptures*, exh. cat., p. 24.
5. Ibid., p. 84.
6. Genesis 19:32.
7. John Coplans, "George Segal: An Interview," p. 4.
8. Minneapolis, 1978, *George Segal*, p. 24.
9. George Segal, "Postscript 1974: Then to Israel," in Van Der Marck, *George Segal*, p. 67.
10. Chicago, Museum of Contemporary Art, 1968, introduction to *George Segal: 12 Human Situations*, exh. cat., n. pag.
11. John Coplans, "George Segal: An Interview," p. 4.

19 David Smith

1. Cleve Gray, *David Smith by David Smith*, p. 134.
2. New York, 1969, *David Smith*, exh. cat., p. 12 and passim.
3. Ibid., p. 156.
4. Interview with Thomas B. Hess in New York, 1964, *David Smith*, exh. cat., n. pag.
5. Its maximum depth is only 17 inches, apart from the square base of 21¾ inches.
6. In the summer of 1959, the artist held a one-man exhibition of his paintings at French and Co., New York City. In April 1976, M. Knoedler and Co. Inc., New York City, exhibited Smith's black and white brush drawings and the stencil drawings.
7. Spoken at a symposium conducted by A. C. Ritchie at The Museum of Modern Art on "The New Sculpture" in February 1952; cited by Rosalind E. Krauss, "Changing the Work of David Smith," p. 32.
8. Jane Harrison Cone, "David Smith," p. 73.
9. Hilton Kramer, "David Smith: Stencils for Sculpture," pp. 41–42; and review of David Smith exhibition at M. Knoedler and Co. Inc., *New York Times*, April 30, 1976.
10. It was shown at the Rijksmuseum Kröller-Müller, Otterlo; the Tate Gallery, London; Kunsthalle, Basel; Kunsthalle, Nürnberg; and the Wilhelm Lehmbruck Museum in Duisberg, Germany.

20 Tony Smith

1. Hartford, Connecticut, 1966, and Philadelphia, 1966–1967, *Tony Smith: Two Exhibitions of Sculpture*, exh. cat., n. pag.
2. Letter to the author, January 20, 1975.
3. Newark, New Jersey, 1969, *Tony Smith: Recent Sculptures*, exh. cat., n. pag.

21 Kenneth Snelson

1. In 1948–1949, Snelson, stimulated by the teaching of Buckminster Fuller at Black Mountain College, executed a group of small-scale experimental sculpture/structures. During the course of these experiments involving solid elements suspending one another in space only by means of tension members, he devised his "X modular form" of two compression elements crossing one another. This invention became the cornerstone of a structure of principles dealing with seemingly apparent free floating compression elements that in reality are dependent on support. Later, in 1955, Buckminster Fuller coined the term "Tensegrity" as a nomenclature for this structural system.
2. "Push and Pull in the Park," *Architectural Forum*, January 1969, pp. 68–69. In this anonymous review of Snelson's first extensive outdoor exhibition of monumental works in New York City in 1968–1969, the writer quotes the artist as follows: "The conflict between tension and compression resolved in a closed system is concisely what it is all about."
3. Letter to the author, September 27, 1976.
4. Stephen A. Kurtz, "Kenneth Snelson: The Elegant Solution," p. 51.
5. In addition to Snelson's achievement in the evolution of tensegrity sculpture, he has also seriously concerned himself with hypotheses dealing with the structure of the atom and has fabricated models exploring its theoretical physical nature. These are works of art in themselves. Arising from his experiments with tensile structures, and studied concurrently with them, Snelson's model and proposals about the nature of atomic form and structure were first published in 1963 and later patented as a matter of permanent record. See Kenneth Snelson, "A Design for the Atom," *Industrial Design Magazine*, February 1963, *Model for Atomic Forms*, U. S. Patent 3276148, October 1966 and Patent 4,009,339, July 11, 1978. Stephen Kurtz points out that Snelson's scientific investigations are, for him, aesthetic exploration and that "his aesthetic is so bound to his vision of the structure of the universe that the two become inseparable" (Kurtz, "Kenneth Snelson," p. 48).
6. Snelson is represented in The Museum of Modern Art and The Whitney Museum of American Art in New York; the Art Institute of Chicago; Albright-Knox Art Gallery, Buffalo; the Hirshhorn Museum and Sculpture Garden, Washington, D.C.; the Storm King Art Center, Mountainville, New York; the Kröller-Müller and Stedelijk Rijksmuseums in Otterlo and Amsterdam; and the city collections of Hanover, Hamburg, Baltimore, Buffalo, and Iowa City.

Appendix 1 Conservation of Outdoor Sculptures

1. Henry Leidheiser, Jr., *The Corrosion of Copper, Tin, and Their Alloys* (Huntington, New York: Robert E. Krieger Publishing Co., Inc., 1979), pp. 77–89.
2. Ibid., pp. 14–22.

3. Herbert H. Uhlig, *Corrosion and Corrosion Control* (New York, London, Sydney, and Toronto: John Wiley and Sons Inc., 1971) pp. 164–175.

4. Reg Butler's letter to Youngja L. Kim, October 8, 1980.

5. Youngja L. Kim, "The Conservation of Jacques Lipchitz's 'Song of the Vowels,'" AIC Fifth Annual Meeting, Boston (Preprints, June 1977), pp. 83–91.

6. Arnaldo Pomodoro's letter to Patrick J. Kelleher, March 2, 1977.

7. George Segal's letter to Youngja L. Kim, September 11, 1980.

8. United States Steel, *USS Cor-Ten for Architectural Applications* (Pittsburgh, 1976), pp. 1–16.

9. Clement Meadmore's letter to Youngja L. Kim, August 7, 1980.

10. Youngja L. Kim, "Problems in Cor-Ten Steel Sculpture," AIC Seventh Annual Meeting, Toronto (Preprints, June 1979), pp. 59–63.

11. Ibid., pp. 59–66.

12. J. C. Scully, *The Fundamentals of Corrosion* (Oxford, New York, Toronto, Sydney, Paris, and Frankfurt: Pergamon Press, 1978), pp. 131–169.

13. Tony Smith came to The Art Museum on May 17, 1977, to discuss the treatment. He agreed with our suggestion to sandblast and repaint the entire sculpture. He later approved the first paint coat that the University's painters applied before the final coat.

14. W. H. Dennis, *Foundations of Iron and Steel Metallurgy* (Amsterdam, London, and New York: Elsvier Publishing Co. Ltd., 1967), pp. 227–231.

15. T. Stambolov, *The Corrosion and Conservation of Metallic Antiquities and Works of Art* (Amsterdam: Central Research Laboratory for Objects of Art and Science), pp. 7–23.

16. R. J. Schaffer, *The Weathering of Natural Building Stones* (London: His Majestey's Sationary Office, 1932), pp. 26–72.

Appendix 2 Picasso's Collaborator: Carl Nesjar

1. For illustrations see Werner Spies, *Picasso Sculpture*, pp. 262–264, 294, 297–298.

2. Artist's notes to author (undated—probably ca. January 1976).

A. Harry Bertoia (American, born in 1915)
The World
Bronze, Height: 55 inches   Commissioned in 1964
Location: Lobby of Woodrow Wilson School of
Public and International Affairs

B. Antoine Bourdelle (French, 1861–1929)
Poet and Pegasus
Bronze relief, 1913; 30 1/2 × 64 inches
(Designed for Elysée Palace Theater, Paris)
Gift of J. Lionberger Davis, Class of 1900
Location: McCormick Hall, outdoor thruway

C. A. Sterling Calder (American, 1870–1945)
1. *Fame* (The Student-Warrior)
Lead, 1923; Height: undetermined (under lifesize)
Location: Tower of 1904 Henry Hall
2. *St. George Slaying the Dragon*
Lead, 1923; Height: undetermined (under lifesize)
Location: 1904 Henry Hall
3. *St. Michael Transfixing the Dragon*
Lead, 1923; Height: undetermined (under lifesize)
Location: 1905 Foulke Hall

D. James E. Davis, Class of 1923
(American, 1901–1974)
Suspended and Revolving Sculpture
Painted aluminum; Height: about 9 feet
Commissioned for The Art Museum in 1966
Location: Entrance lobby of School of Engineering
and Applied Sciences

E. Sir Jacob Epstein (British, 1880–1959)
St. Michael
Gilded plaster, 1958; Height: 47 1/4 inches
Fragment from original plaster for *St. Michael and
the Devil* on Coventry Cathedral, England
Gift of Lady Epstein
Location: South transept of University Chapel

F. James Fitzgerald (American, born in 1910)
Fountain of Freedom
Bronze; Height: 23 feet   Commissioned in 1966
Location: Woodrow Wilson School of Public
and International Affairs

G. Dimitri Hadzi (American, born in 1921)
1. *Centaur with Pipes*
Bronze, 1954–1971; Height: 8 feet 10 inches
Gift of Brian T. Leeb, Class of 1918, and Mrs. Leeb
in honor of President and Mrs. Robert F. Goheen
Location: Garden pool at Prospect
2. *Thermopylae*
Bronze, 1961, no. 3/4; Height: 45 inches
Gift of Stephen F. Vorhees, Class of 1900
Location: Interior court of School of Engineering
and Applied Sciences

H. Rudolph Hoflehner (Austrian, born in 1916)
Condition Humaine
Iron, 1960; Height: 8 feet
Gift of Stanley J. Seeger, Jr., Class of 1952
Purchased from *XXX Biennale di Venezia* (1960)
Location: Front green of McCormick Hall Annex

I. Bernard Rosenthal (American, born in 1914)
Palimpsest II
Black aluminum relief, 1959; 84 × 40 inches
Gift of Stanley J. Seeger, Jr., Class of 1952
Location: B-Floor stacks of Firestone Library

J. David Savage (American, born in 1923)
Equation
Stainless steel, 1969; Height: 7 feet 8 inches
Gift of Mrs. R. Woolcott Hooker
Location: Underground inner court of
Firestone Library

K. Julius Schmidt (American, born in 1929)
Untitled
Bronze, 1968; Height: 37 inches
Gift of the Friends of The Art Museum
Location: Whig Hall

L. Alberto Viani (Italian, born in 1906)
1. *Caryatid*
Black Carrara marble, 1952; Height: 46 inches
Gift of the Friends of The Art Museum
Location: Entrance lobby of School of Engineering
and Applied Sciences
2. *Nudo*
Brazen bronze, 1960; Height: 6 feet 4 inches
Gift of Stanley J. Seeger, Jr., Class of 1952
Location: A-Floor reading room of Firestone Library

Bibliography

General Reference

Arnason, H. H. *History of Modern Art*. New York: Harry N. Abrams, 1968.

Burnham, Jack. *Beyond Modern Sculpture*. New York: G. Braziller, 1968.

Goldwater, Robert. *What is Modern Sculpture?* New York: The Museum of Modern Art, 1969.

Herbert, Robert, ed. *Modern Artists on Art*. Englewood Cliffs, N.J.: Prentice-Hall, 1964.

Hunter, Sam. *American Art of the Twentieth Century*. New York: Harry N. Abrams, 1972.

New York, 1976. The Whitney Museum of American Art. *200 Years of American Sculpture*. Exh. cat. Essays by various authors. New York: David R. Godine, 1976.

Read, Herbert. *A Concise History of Modern Sculpture*. New York: Praeger Publishers, 1964.

Putnam Collection

Cabutti, Lucio. "Sculpture in a University." *Bolaffiarte*, No. 65 (December 1976–January 1977), pp. 54–57.

Cameron, Gledhill. "Princeton Campus Home for Art: Million Dollar Donation Used." *The Evening Times* (Trenton, New Jersey), October 4, 1969.

_____. "Sculpture Tip Toes in at Princeton." *The Evening Times*, January 7, 1970.

_____. "Campus Will Be Outdoor Museum." *Princeton Packet*, December 13, 1969.

Fenton, John M. "The Putnam Sculptures." *Princeton Alumni Weekly*, December 14, 1971, pp. 6–13.

Friend, Miriam. "Modern Sculpture Turns Campus into Outdoor Art Museum." *The Packet Magazine*, August 1971, pp. 13–21.

Genauer, Emily. "Art and the Artist." *New York Post Magazine*, December 23, 1972, p. 14.

_____. "Princeton Placing $1 Million in Sculpture Gifts." *New York Times*, December 26, 1969.

_____. "Princeton Plans Permanent Sculpture Display." *Town Topics* (Princeton, New Jersey), December 18, 1969.

_____. "The Putnam Sculptures: 20th Century Masterpieces Give Dramatic Perspectives to Princeton's Familiar Vistas." *Princeton Alumni Weekly*, January 27, 1970, pp. 12–15.

Reg Butler

Louisville, Kentucky, 1963. J. B. Speed Art Museum. *Reg Butler: A Retrospective Exhibition*. Exh. cat. by A. Franklin Page. Louisville: J. B. Speed Art Museum, 1963. Extensive bibliography.

New York, 1955. Curt Valentin Gallery. *Reg Butler*. Exh. cat. Introduction by Roland Penrose. New York: Curt Valentin Gallery, 1955.

New York, 1962. Pierre Matisse Gallery. *Reg Butler: Recent Sculpture (1959–1962)*. Exh. cat. with letter to A. F. Page from the artist. New York: Pierre Matisse Gallery, 1962.

New York, 1973. Pierre Matisse Gallery. *Reg Butler: Sculpture and Drawings, 1968–1972*. Exh. cat. Introduction by John Russell. New York: Pierre Matisse Gallery, 1973.

Ritchie, Andrew C. *The New Decade: 22 European Painters and Sculptors*. New York: The Museum of Modern Art, 1955, pp 65–69.

Selz, Peter. *New Images of Man*. New York: The Museum of Modern Art, 1959, pp. 33–34.

Alexander Calder

Arnason, H. H., and Guerrero, Pedro E. *Calder*. Princeton, N.J.: Van Nostrand, 1966.

Calder, Alexander. *Calder: An Autobiography with Pictures*. New York: Pantheon Books, 1966.

Chicago, 1974. Museum of Contemporary Art. *Alexander Calder: A Retrospective Exhibition, Works from 1925 to 1974*. Exh. cat. by Albert E. Elsen. Chicago: Museum of Contemporary Art, 1974.

Lipman, Jean. *Calder's Universe*. New York: Viking Press in cooperation with The Whitney Museum of American Art, 1976. Complete bibliography.

Osborn, Robert. "Calder's International Monuments." *Art in America*, 57, No. 2 (March–April 1969), pp. 32–49.

Russell, John. "Alexander Calder, Leading U.S. Artist, Dies." *New York Times*, November 12, 1976, pp. A1, D14.

Saint-Paul-de-Vence, France, 1969. Fondation Maeght. *Calder.* Exh. cat. by James Johnson Sweeney et al. Saint-Paul-de-Vence, France: Fondation Maeght, 1969.

Sir Jacob Epstein

Black, Robert. *The Art of Jacob Epstein.* Cleveland, Ohio: World Publishing Co., 1942.

Buckle, Richard. *Jacob Epstein: Sculptor.* London: Faber and Faber Ltd., 1963.

Epstein, Jacob. *Let There Be Sculpture.* New York: G.P. Putnam's Sons, 1940.

London, 1961. The Tate Gallery. *Epstein.* Exh. cat. Introduction by Sir John Rothenstein. London: Arts Council of Great Britain, 1961.

Naum Gabo

Gabo, Naum. *Gabo. Realistic Manifesto* and other writings of Gabo. Introductory essays by Sir Herbert Read and Sir Leslie Martin. London: Lund Humphries, 1957.

_____. *Gabo.* London: Lund Humphries, 1957.

_____. *Of Divers Arts.* Bollingen Series, No. 35. The A. W. Mellon Lectures in Fine Arts. New York: Pantheon Books, 1962.

New York, 1948. The Museum of Modern Art. *Naum Gabo/Antoine Pevsner.* Exh. cat. Introduction by Sir Herbert Read, text by Ruth Olsen and Abraham Chanin. New York: The Museum of Modern Art, 1948.

Paris, 1971. Musée National d'Art Moderne. *Naum Gabo.* Exh. cat. Introduction by Maurice Besset. Paris: Musée National d'Art Moderne, 1971.

Rickey, George. *Constructivism: Origins and Evolution.* New York: G. Braziller, 1967.

Michael Hall

Chicago, 1974. Grant Park. *Sculpture in the Park.* Exh. cat. Chicago: Auxiliary Board of the Art Institute of Chicago, 1974.

Grand Rapids, Michigan, 1973. Grand Rapids Art Museum. *Sculpture off the Pedestal.* Exh. cat. Introduction by Fred A. Myers and essays by Barbara Rose. Grand Rapids: Grand Rapids Art Museum, 1973.

Hall, Michael. "The Bronze Caster: Alchemist Artist." *Accent Magazine*, 2, No. 1 (October 1967).

_____. "Sculpture—Where It Was and Where It Is." *Cranbrook Magazine*, 2, No. 2 (Winter 1971).

Hieronymus, Clara. "Old Gym's New Mastodons." *The Nashville Tennessean*, March 3, 1968, pp. D–1, 3.

Nashville, Tennessee, 1968. Vanderbilt University Gallery. *Mastodon: Recent Sculpture by Michael Hall.* Exh. cat. Nashville: Vanderbilt University, 1968.

Gaston Lachaise

Gallatin, A. E. *Gaston Lachaise.* New York: E. P. Dutton and Co., 1924.

Ithaca, New York, 1974. Herbert F. Johnson Museum of Art, Cornell University. *Gaston Lachaise, 1882–1935.* Exh. cat. by Gerald Nordland. Ithaca: Cornell University, 1974.

Kramer, Hilton. *The Sculpture of Gaston Lachaise.* Essays by Hart Crane and others. New York: Eakins Press Publishers, 1967.

Lachaise, Gaston. "A Comment on My Sculpture." *Creative Art*, 3 (August 1928), xxii–xxvi.

Los Angeles, 1964. Los Angeles County Museum of Art. *Gaston Lachaise, 1882–1935; Sculpture and Drawings.* Exh. cat. by Gerald Nordland. Los Angeles: Los Angeles County Museum of Art, 1964. Also shown at The Whitney Museum of American Art, New York.

New York, 1935. The Museum of Modern Art. *Gaston Lachaise: Retrospective Exhibition.* Exh. cat. by Lincoln Kirstein. New York: W. E. Rudge's Sons, 1935.

New York, 1947. M. Knoedler and Co. *Gaston Lachaise (1882–1935).* Exh. cat. Essays by Lincoln Kirstein, e. e. Cummings, and A. Hyatt Mayor. New York: M. Knoedler and Co., 1947.

Nordland, Gerald. *Gaston Lachaise: The Man and His Work.* New York: G. Braziller, 1974.

Jacques Lipchitz

Arnason, H. H. *Jacques Lipchitz: Sketches in Bronze.* New York: Praeger Publishers, 1969.

Goldwater, Robert. *Lipchitz.* London: Zwemmer, 1958.

Hammacher, A. M. *Jacques Lipchitz: His Sculpture.* New York: Harry N. Abrams, Inc., 1975.

Hope, Henry R. *The Sculpture of Jacques Lipchitz.* New York: The Museum of Modern Art, 1954.

Lipchitz, Jacques, with Arnason, H. H. *My Life in Sculpture.* Documents of 20th-Century Art. New York: Viking Press, 1972. Extensive bibliography.

Patai, Irene. *Encounters: The Life of Jacques Lipchitz.* Foreword by Andrew C. Ritchie. New York: Funk and Wagnalls Co., 1961.

Clement Meadmore

Davies, Hugh M. "Clement Meadmore." *Arts Magazine,* March 1977, p. 7.

Grand Rapids, Michigan, 1973. Grand Rapids Art Museum. *Sculpture Off the Pedestal.* Exh. cat. Introduction by Fred A. Myers and essays by Barbara Rose. Grand Rapids: Grand Rapids Art Museum, 1973.

Hughes, Robert. "Solid Man." *Time,* April 5, 1971, p. 66.

McCaughey, Patrick. "The Monolith and Modernist Sculpture." *Art International,* 14 (November 19, 1970), pp. 19–24.

Meadmore, Clement; Fry, Edward; and Rose, Barbara. "Symposium on Three Dimensions." *Arts Magazine,* 49 (January 1975), pp. 62–65.

Siegel, Jeanne, "Clement Meadmore: Circling The Square." *Art News,* 70, No. 10 (February 1972), pp. 56–59.

Henry Moore

Argan, Giulio Carlo. *Henry Moore.* Translated by Daniel Dichter. New York: Harry N. Abrams, Inc., 1973.

Carandente, Giovanni, ed. *Henry Moore.* Cat. no. 160. Catalogo della Mostra Firenze-Forte di Belvedere, May–September 1972.

Geneva, 1970–1971. Galerie Gérald Cramer. *Elephant Skull: Original Etchings by Henry Moore.* Exh. cat. Foreword by Alistair Grant. Geneva: Galerie Gérald Cramer, 1970.

James, Philip. *Henry Moore on Sculpture.* London: Macdonald, 1966.

London, 1968. The Tate Gallery. *Henry Moore Exhibition.* Exh. cat. by David Sylvester. London: The Arts Council of Great Britain, 1968.

Melville, Robert, ed. *Henry Moore: Sculpture and Drawing (1921–1969).* London: Thames and Hudson, 1970.

Read, Herbert. *Henry Moore, Sculptor.* London: A. Zwemmer, 1934.

Russell, John. *Henry Moore.* London: Lane, 1968.

Seldis, Henry J. *Henry Moore in America.* New York: Praeger Publishers in association with the Los Angeles County Museum of Art, 1973.

Sweeney, James Johnson. *Henry Moore.* New York: The Museum of Modern Art, 1946.

Sylvester, David, and Bowness, Alan, eds. *Henry Moore, Sculpture and Drawings.* Introduction by Sir Herbert Read. 4 vols. London: P. Lund, Humphries, 1957–1975.

Masayuki Nagare

Baker, A. T. "Please Touch." *Time,* December 3, 1973, 113.

New York, 1963. Staempfli Gallery. *Masayuki Nagare: Recent Sculpture.* Exh. cat. by George W. Staempfli. New York: Staempfli Gallery, 1963.

New York, 1965. Staempfli Gallery. *Recent Sculpture of Masayuki Nagare.* Exh. cat. by Gordon Bailey Washburn. Tokyo: John Weatherhill, Inc., 1965.

New York, 1973. Staempfli Gallery. *Masayuki Nagare.* Exh. cat. by George W. Staempfli. New York: Staempfli Gallery, 1973.

San Francisco, 1967. San Francisco Museum of Art. *Masayuki Nagare.* Exh. cat. by George W. Staempfli. Berne: Staempfli and Co., 1967. Also shown at the Arts Club of Chicago and the Staempfli Gallery, New York, 1968.

Louise Nevelson

Glimcher, Arnold B. *Louise Nevelson*. New York: Praeger Publishers, 1972.

Gordon, John. *Louise Nevelson*. New York: Praeger Publishers for The Whitney Museum of American Art, 1967.

Minneapolis, 1973. Walker Art Center. *Nevelson: Wood Sculptures*. Exh. cat. by Martin Friedman. New York: E. P. Dutton and Co., Inc., 1973. Also shown at the San Francisco Museum of Art, the Dallas Museum of Fine Arts, the High Museum of Art (Atlanta), the William Rockhill Nelson Gallery of Art (Kansas City), and the Cleveland Museum of Art.

Nemser, Cindy. "Louise Nevelson." *In Art-Talk: Conversations with Twelve Women Artists*, pp. 52–70. New York: Charles Scribner's Sons, 1975.

Nevelson, Louise. *Dawns and Dusks*. Taped conversations with Diana MacKown. New York: Charles Scribner's Sons, 1976.

Otterlo, The Netherlands, 1969. Rijksmuseum Kröller-Müller. *Louise Nevelson: Sculpture 1959–69*. Exh. cat. Introduction by R. W. D. Oxenaar. Hilversum: Steendrukkerij De Jong, 1969.

Roberts, Collette. *Nevelson*. Paris: the Pocket Museums, Editions Georges Fall, 1964.

Isamu Noguchi

Forgey, Banjamin. "Isamu Noguchi's Elegant World of Space and Function." *Smithsonian*, 9 (April 1978), cover and pp. 46–54.

Gordon, John. *Isamu Noguchi*. New York: Praeger Publishers for The Whitney Museum of American Art, 1968.

Gruen, John. "The Artist Speaks: Isamu Noguchi." *Art in America*, 56 (March–April 1968), cover and pp. 28–31.

Hess, Thomas B. "Isamu Noguchi '46." *Art News*, 45 (September 1946), pp. 34–38, 47, 50–51.

Hunter, Sam. *Isamu Noguchi*. New York: Abbeville Press, Inc., 1978.

Noguchi, Isamu. "Meanings in Modern Sculpture." *Art News*, 48 (March 1949), 12–15.

———. *A Sculptor's World*. Forward by R. Buckminster Fuller. New York: Harper and Row, 1968.

Robertson, Bryan. *Noguchi: Steel Sculptures*. New York: Pace Editions, 1975.

Wolfe, Ruth. "Noguchi: Past, Present, Future." *Art in America*, 56 (March–April 1968), pp. 32–45.

Eduardo Paolozzi

Finch, Christopher. "Paolozzi in the Sixties." *Art International*, 10, No. 9 (1966), p. 25ff.

Hanover, 1974. Kestner-Gesellschaft. *Eduardo Paolozzi*. Exh. cat. Foreword by Carl-Albrecht Haenlein, essays by Paolozzi and others. Hanover: Kestner-Gesellschaft, 1974.

Kirkpatrick, Diane. *Eduardo Paolozzi*. Greenwich, Connecticut: New York Graphic Society, 1970.

London, 1966. Robert Fraser Gallery. *Eduardo Paolozzi: A Selection of Works from 1963–66*. Exh. cat. London: Robert Fraser Gallery, 1966. Also shown at the Pace Gallery, New York.

London, 1971. The Tate Gallery. *Eduardo Paolozzi*. Exh. cat. Forward by Norman Reid, essay by Frank Witford. Boston: Boston Book and Art Publisher, 1971.

Paolozzi, Eduardo. *Kex*. Chicago: William and Noma Copley Foundation, 1966.

Reichardt, Jasia. "Eduardo Paolozzi." *Studio International*, 168 (October 1964), pp. 152–156.

Russell, John. *Pop Art Redefined*. London: Thames and Hudson, 1969.

Schneede, Uwe M. *Eduardo Paolozzi*. Translated by W. Woodson Hard. London: Thames and Hudson, 1971.

Selz, Peter. *New Images of Man*. New York: The Museum of Modern Art, 1959, pp. 117–122.

Antoine Pevsner

Massat, René. *Antoine Pevsner et le constructivisme*. Preface by Jean Cassou. Paris: Caractères, 1956.

New York, 1948. The Museum of Modern Art. *Naum Gabo/Antoine Pevsner*. Exh. cat. Introduction by Herbert Read, text by Ruth Olsen and Abraham Chanin. New York: The Museum of Modern Art, 1948.

Paris, 1956–1957. Musée National d'Art Moderne. *Antoine Pevsner*. Exh. cat. Introduction by Jean Cassou, text by Bernard Dorival. Paris: Editions des Musée Nationaux, 1956–1957.

Peissi, Pierre. *Antoine Pevsner: Tribute by a Friend.* Essay by Carola Giedeon-Welcker, "Antoine Pevsner's Spatial Imagination." Neuchâtel, Switzerland: Editions du Griffon, 1961.

Pablo Picasso

Kahnweiler, Daniel-Henry. *Les sculptures de Picasso.* Photographs by Brassai. Paris: Editions du Chêne, 1949.

Langert, Olle, and Edwards, Folke. "Picasso—Monument." *Paletten* (Göteborg, Sweden), No. 2 (1971), pp. 24–29.

New York, 1967. The Museum of Modern Art. *The Sculpture of Picasso*. Exh. cat. No. 151. Essay by Roland Penrose. New York: The Museum of Modern Art, 1967.

Paris, 1966. Galerie Jeanne Bucher. *Picasso et le béton*. Exh. cat. by Daniel Gervis. Paris: Galerie Jeanne Bucher, 1966.

Parmelin, Hélène. *Picasso—Women (1954–1963): Cannes and Mougins.* Paris: Editions Cercle d'Art, 1963.

Penrose, Roland. *Picasso.* London: Zwemmer, 1961.
————. *The Sculpture of Picasso.* New York: The Museum of Modern Art, 1967.

Shirey, David L. "The New Girl at Princeton: A Sculpture by Picasso." *New York Times*, November 5, 1971, p. 32.

Spies, Werner. *Picasso Sculpture: With a Complete Catalog.* Translated by J. Maxwell Brownjohn. London: Thames and Hudson, 1972.

"'Totem': The Talk of the Town." *The New Yorker*, January 8, 1972, pp. 25–26.

Arnaldo Pomodoro

Dorfles, Gillo. "Arnaldo Pomodoro: Sculptor of the Cosmos." *Studio International Art* (London), 167 (April 1964), pp. 140–145.

Libro per le sculture di Arnaldo Pomodoro. Introduction by Sam Hunter; Ugo Mulas, Francesco Leonetti, Guido Ballo, Alberto Boatto, and Gillo Dorfles, collaborators. Milan: Gabriele Mazzotta, 1974.

London, 1968. Marlborough New London Gallery, 1968.

Milan, 1974. Rotonda di via Besana. *Arnaldo Pomodoro*. Exh. cat. Introduction and interview by Sam Hunter, essay by Franco Russoli. Milan: Amilcare Pizzi, 1974. Extensive bibliography.

New York, 1965. Marlborough-Gerson Gallery. *Arnaldo Pomodoro*. Exh. cat. New York: Marlborough-Gerson Gallery, 1965.

Pesaro, Italy, 1971. Museo Civico. *Arnaldo Pomodoro: Sculture nella città*. Exh. cat. Essay by Guido Ballo. Pesaro: Museo Civico, 1971.

Pomodoro, Arnaldo. Interview with Mila Pistoi at the Venice Biennale in 1964. Published in *Review Marcatre* (Milan), Nos. 8–10 (1964), pp. 240–241.

Rotterdam, 1969. Museum Boymans-van Beuningen. *Arnaldo Pomodoro*. Exh. cat. Essay, "Notes on my Work Since 1966," by Arnaldo Pomodoro. Rotterdam: Museum Boymans-van Beuningen, 1969.

George Rickey

Los Angeles, 1972. University of California at Los Angeles Art Galleries. *George Rickey: Retrospective Exhibition*. Exh. cat. Interview with George Rickey by Frederick S. Wight. Los Angeles: University of California at Los Angeles Arts Council, 1972.

New York, 1971. Staempfli Gallery. *George Rickey: Recent Sculpture*. Exh. cat. Essay by George Rickey, "Surfaces and Volumes." New York: Staempfli Gallery, 1971.

Rickey, George. *Constructivism: Origins and Evolution*. New York: G. Braziller, 1967.

_____. "The Morphology of Movement: A Study of Kinetic Art." *Art Journal*, 22/4 (Summer 1963), p. 220ff.

Washington, D.C., 1966. Corcoran Gallery of Art. *George Rickey: Sixteen Years of Kinetic Art*. Exh. cat. by Peter Selz. Berne: Staempfli and Co., 1966.

George Segal

Chicago, 1968. Museum of Contemporary Art. *George Segal: 12 Human Situations*. Exh. cat. by Jan Van Der Marck.

Long Beach, California, 1977. The Art Galleries, California State University. *George Segal: Pastels 1957–1965*. Exh. cat. by Constance W. Glenn.

Minneapolis, 1978. Walker Art Center. *George Segal: Sculptures*. Exh. cat. by Martin Friedman and Graham W. J. Beal.

Philadelphia, 1976. Institute of Contemporary Art, University of Pennsylvania. *George Segal: Environments*. Exh. cat. by Jose L. Barrio-Garay.

Seitz, William C. *Segal*. New York: Harry N. Abrams, 1972.

Van Der Marck, Jan. *George Segal*. New York: Harry N. Abrams, 1975.

David Smith

Cambridge, Massachusetts, 1966. Fogg Art Museum, Harvard University. *David Smith, 1906–1965: A Retrospective Exhibition*. Exh. cat. by Jane Harrison Cone. Cambridge: Harvard University, 1966. Also shown at the Washington Gallery of Modern Art.

Cone, Jane Harrison. "David Smith." *Artforum*, 5, No. 10 (1967), pp. 72–78.

Gray, Cleve, ed. *David Smith by David Smith*. New York: Holt, Rinehart and Winston, New York, 1968.

Hunter, Sam. "David Smith." *The Museum of Modern Art Bulletin*, 25, No. 1 (1957), pp. 3–36.

Kramer, Hilton. "David Smith: Stencils for Sculpture." *Art in America*, 50, No. 4 (1962).

Krauss, Rosalind E. "Changing the Work of David Smith." *Art in America*, 62 (September 1974), pp. 30–34.

_____. *Terminal Iron Works: The Sculpture of David Smith*. Cambridge, Massachusetts: MIT Press, 1971.

McCoy, Garnett, ed. *David Smith*. Speeches, formal writings, interviews, letters, and notes. New York: Praeger Publishers, 1973.

New York, 1946. The Buchholz and Willard Galleries. *The Sculpture of David Smith*. Exh. cat. by W. R. Valentiner. New York: The Buchholz and Willard Galleries, 1946.

New York, 1964. Marlborough-Gerson Gallery. *David Smith*. Exh. cat. New York: Marlborough-Gerson Gallery, 1964.

New York, 1969. The Solomon R. Guggenheim Museum. *David Smith*. Exh. cat. by Edward F. Fry. New York: The Solomon R. Guggenheim Museum, 1969.

Philadelphia, 1964. Institute of Contemporary Art. *David Smith: Sculpture and Drawings*. Introduction by Clement Greenberg. Philadelphia: Institute of Contemporary Art, 1964.

Russell, John. "David Smith's Art Is Best Revealed in Natural Settings." *Smithsonian*, March 1977, pp. 68–74.

Tony Smith

Baro, Gene. "Tony Smith: Toward Speculation in Pure Form." *Art International*, 11 (Summer 1967), pp. 27–31.

Burton, Scott. "Old Master at the New Frontier." *Art News*, 65 (December 1966), pp. 52–55, 68–70.

College Park, Maryland, 1974. University of Maryland Art Gallery. *Tony Smith: Painting and Sculpture*. Exh. cat. Foreword by Eleanor Green. College Park: University of Maryland Art Gallery, 1974.

Hartford, Connecticut, 1966 and Philadelphia, 1966–1967. Wadsworth Atheneum and Institute of Contemporary Art. *Tony Smith: Two Exhibitions of Sculpture*. Exh. cat. Introduction by Sam Wagstaff, Jr. Hartford: Wadsworth Atheneum, 1966.

Lippard, Lucy R. *Tony Smith*. London: Thames and Hudson, 1972.

Newark, 1970. Newark Museum. *Seven Sculptures by Tony Smith*. Exh. cat. Introduction by Eugene C. Goossen. Newark: New Jersey State Council on the Arts, 1970. Also shown at the Montclair Art Museum; The Art Museum, Princeton University; and the New Jersey State Museum, Trenton.

New York, 1970. M. Knoedler and Co. *Tony Smith: Recent Sculptures*. Exh. cat. Foreword by Martin Friedman and interview by Lucy Lippard. New York: M. Knoedler and Co., 1971.

Wagstaff, Sam, Jr. "Talking with Tony Smith." *Artforum*, 5 (December 1966), pp. 14–19.

Kenneth Snelson

Battcock, Gregory. "Kenneth Snelson: Dialogue Between Stress and Tension at the Dwan." *Arts Magazine*, 42, No. 4 (February 1968), pp. 27–29.

Coplans, John. "An Interview with Kenneth Snelson." *Artform*, 5 (March 1967), pp. 46–49.

Donadio, Emmie. "Kenneth Snelson." *Arts Magazine*, 49 (February 1975), p. 25.

Hanover, 1971. Kunstverein Hannover. *Kenneth Snelson*. Exh. cat. Essay, "Struktur und Spannung," by Lazlo Glozer. Hanover: Kunstverein Hannover, 1971.

Kurtz, Stephen A. "Kenneth Snelson: The Elegant Solution." *Art News*, 67, No. 6 (October 1968), pp. 48–51.

Munich, 1975. Galerie Buchholz. *Kenneth Snelson*. Exh. cat. Munich: Galerie Buchholz, 1975.

New York, 1979. Zabriskie Gallery, *Kenneth Snelson*. Exh. cat. October 30–December 21, 1979.

"Push and Pull in the Park." *Architectural Forum*, January 1969, pp. 68–69.

Snelson, Kenneth. "A Design for the Atom." *Industrial Design*, February 1963.

———. "How Primary is Structure." *Art Voices*, Summer 1966.

———. *Portrait of an Atom*. Exh. cat. Baltimore: Maryland Science Center, 1981.

Whelan, Richard. "Kenneth Snelson: Straddling the Abyss Between Art and Science." *Art News*, 80, No. 2 (February 1981), pp. 68–73.